JACOB RAPOO TLHAGALE

TURNING A CRISIS INTO AN OPPORTUNITY

JACOB RAPOO TLHAGALE

TURNING A CRISIS INTO AN OPPORTUNITY

A NEVER SURRENDERING SPIRIT IS THE PANACEA TO A LIFE'S CRISES -THAT WILL HELP IN TURNING A CRISIS INTO AN OPPORTUNITY

Blessed Hope Publishing

Imprint
Any brand names and product names mentioned in this book are subject to trademark, brand or patent protection and are trademarks or registered trademarks of their respective holders. The use of brand names, product names, common names, trade names, product descriptions etc. even without a particular marking in this work is in no way to be construed to mean that such names may be regarded as unrestricted in respect of trademark and brand protection legislation and could thus be used by anyone.

Cover image: www.ingimage.com

Publisher:
Blessed Hope Publishing
is a trademark of
International Book Market Service Ltd., member of OmniScriptum Publishing Group
17 Meldrum Street, Beau Bassin 71504, Mauritius
Printed at: see last page
ISBN: 978-613-7-96547-4

Tittle:"TURNING CRISIS INTO OPPORTUNITY

Crises come into our lives, no matter how we may try to avoid them. They are troubling, unwanted experiences or events that take us way out of our comfort zone. Typically, crises result in some type of loss. The very nature of a crisis is antithetical to our core values of certainty and predictability as they vanish in an instant.

We desperately try to restore order to our lives, as chaos seems to prevail. Yet, if we learn to reframe how we see crisis, we might actually take advantage of it. There is the potential for alchemy as the crisis unfolds into a gain, provided we learn to stop resisting the unwanted change.

The crisis may be of a financial, relationship, health, or spiritual nature. Those crises that are internally driven tend to be relational, psychological, or emotional. Ordinarily, we try to avoid these upsets as best we can. Yet, upheavals are at times leveled upon us and may not be of our making. We may feel like victims of the circumstances, as we struggle to hold on to life as we knew it.

Typically, personal change requires our motivation and intention to serve as the catalyst to power the transition. Crisis, on the other hand, removes the self-motivating requirement as it places us squarely outside of our familiar zone. The crisis literally removes the boundaries that have circumscribed us.

It is as if a tornado has swept in, and when we open our eyes, everything has changed. The maelstrom places us well beyond the bounds of the known. We typically find ourselves wanting desperately to get back inside the comfort of the known. But the crisis precludes that option. There is no going back. But that is where the opportunity lies.

1..BREAKING FREE

Growth and fundamental levels of change only tend to occur when we are out of our comfort zone. We can refer to this as being far from equilibrium, where certainty and predictability no longer reign supreme. So we might look at the crisis as a blessing in disguise, albeit an unwanted one.

Steve Jobs might have felt self-defeated and victimized himself after he was fired from Apple many years ago. He chose otherwise. After his dismissal, he grasped the crisis by the horns, seeing opportunity where others did not. He went on to lead a small animation company and turn it into the juggernaut that is now Pixar. When The Walt Disney Company bought Pixar in 2006, Jobs immediately became the largest shareholder in Disney. The moral of the story is that unwanted change happens; look beyond it and embrace the discomfort.

The crisis is but a snapshot of a moment in time, and one we'd prefer to avoid. But to achieve self-empowerment requires looking beyond that snapshot and envisioning what door of potential has just flung open.

The individual whose spouse initiated divorce or left them for another person feels betrayed and perhaps heartsick. After a time, though, they may, in fact, come to feel thankful to be freed from an unworthy and inauthentic relationship. This is particularly true if they evolve through the loss and benefit from a new and healthier relationship.

I fervently believe that every crisis presents an opportunity. Crisis and opportunity are merely different aspects of the process. Do we choose to focus on the crisis and freeze in fear, or do we inquire as to what the opportunity may be? Let's take a deeper look at the phenomena of crisis.

2. ILLUMINATING CRISIS

Crises tend to present themselves as either acute or chronic circumstances. For example, there is an economic upheaval that is driving the United States and the world economy into highly volatile perturbations, with both wealth and employment literally disappearing. In the lives of most people, this is an external crisis raining upon them, typically not of their own making. Yet, through these losses, many people are coming to reflect on their values and choices and are making adjustments—due to the crisis—that actually benefit them.

A high-powered Wall Street executive, with whom I was working, had hardly a spare moment for his family, as he was ever consumed with achieving more and more. The loss of his job at first paralyzed him with fear. After a time, however, he was able to reevaluate his priorities. He now works from home in a small business he founded, and he and his family have greatly benefited.

An unexpected health issue or the death of a loved one may bring anxiety and/or loss. However painful and stressful these challenges and losses may be, the opportunity to be in the moment and value life from a differing perspective can prevail.

Chronic crises are more personal as they manifest thematically throughout one's life. One's relationship struggles or battles with self-esteem or depression tend to recur throughout life. These patterns are perpetual mini-crises awaiting a more fundamental resolution.

Learning to look at the larger themes and patterns that set up these challenges will help develop a vantage point from which you may break through the struggle. In other words, what are the recurring stories of your life? What is your participation in this storyline?

Likewise, relationship difficulties tend to self-perpetuate until a turning point is reached. Often, the relationship crisis launches the couple into new territory, whereby growth may finally be achieved. The pain endured through the crisis may actually enable this gain. For example, infidelity can be a horrific experience, but it may also open the door to a more authentic examination of the marriage and the possibility of a hopeful resolution. I have assisted a number of couples as they worked through this travail and transformed their relationships in a healthy way.

3. WHERE IS THE OPPORTUNITY?

Let's delve a bit deeper into the opportunity that prevails through these hardships. A crisis is defined in Webster's Dictionary as: "a crucial or decisive point or situation; a turning point." If we focus on the phrase "turning point," we might ask ourselves, "Toward where are we turning?"

It is in this non-reactive contemplation that we may elect to seek opportunity. This potentiality becomes obscured when we are mired in the loss of the familiar as opposed to venturing into the new. This tipping point is precisely where transformation occurs.

Do we gaze into the unfolding potential of change, or do we focus on the loss of the familiar? Your answer reveals your relationship between loss and opportunity. Ultimately the question is whether we choose to freeze in the panic of the unfamiliar or we seek to opportunism the new territory that's unfolding for us. The former presents anxiety and retreat, the latter evokes growth. Release your hold on loss and embrace your relationship with opportunity. They are inversely correlated.

The only constant in the universe is flow. What we call crisis is simply the occurrence of change. We are not the masters of change, and if we release our need to control it, we can ride the waves of change and often turn it into opportunity.

The ability to transform a crisis into an opportunity is the hallmark of all successful enterprises that have stood the test of time. Yet today, even the most successful enterprises are facing crises they've never faced before as they compete in a business environment that is being radically transformed by digitization. It may be a crisis of cost pressure or limited capacity, or the inability to meet the needs of the rapidly changing market. Many large enterprises face strategic challenges that relate to a fragmented IT environment with too much overhead and portfolio maintenance to allow for innovation. And yet there is no time to waste. Action is expected now.

In many of these cases, an enterprise must make a dramatic change to its operating model, which can distress employees and threaten the bottom line. People are not sure of their roles. Leaders are not sure how to turn their vision into a reality.

Enterprises addressing big change often operate as if there are only two extreme approaches:

- The methodical approach, which is a step-by-step way to minimize risk but can take a long time with increased cost and transformation fatigue, or
- The rip-the-bandage-off approach, which focuses on the most important tasks and manages risk in a hyper-care manner. This approach is quick and puts less burden on the organization overall, but the increased risk may cause rework, and—even worse—gaps in service that may come with a high cost.

Lois is speaking at the 2015 ISG Sourcing Industry Conference.

In the best of cases, the answer ends up in between the two extremes, with an approach tailored to specific environmental and internal factors.

Here are the Top 5 ways an enterprise can turn a crisis into an opportunity and implement big change:

1. **Focus on the needs of the business and the customer.**
   Address how the change and its related risks will impact the customer. Identify the most critical roles and activities and develop a more methodical approach in those focus areas, along with enhanced organizational change activities.

2. Define the burning need. If you were in IT in the year 1999, there was no doubt that the priority was "Y2K." The same clarity can be created today. Identify your priorities and make them known. Build an enterprise-wide understanding of WHY a change is about to take place, WHY it is best for the company and WHY it's best for the IT organization. Everyone has a role to play in making change. Help make it personal for them.

3. Standardize and integrate processes through an integration platform. Most large enterprises have grown both organically and through mergers and acquisitions. Over time, employees use any number of stopgap solutions to compensate for fragmented and insufficient systems, creating a patchwork of software and manual work-around that make for slow and onerous processes. Implement an integration platform that standardizes processes across verticals and train everyone on the same methods.

4. Build a workforce that offers business-differentiating skills. When an enterprise has a highly tenured workforce, it may become lax, doing things the way they have always been done. This workplace culture can make it difficult to adopt the latest methodologies and emerging technologies. Bring in new and diverse talent to stir in fresh approaches and infuse expertise that may be missing.

5. Create a strong cross-stakeholder program team to make it happen. Involvement from key vocal business stakeholders, service providers and other adjacent organizations such as finance and procurement is essential for decision-making and progress. Also, be sure to take advantage of those who have done this before. Use tried and true methods. There is no gold medal for making it up on your own.

4....SOMETIMES THE WORLD NEEDS A CRISIS: TURNING CHALLENGES INTO OPPORTUNITIES

In a 1959 speech, John F. Kennedy famously said: "When written in Chinese, the word 'crisis' is composed of two characters—one represents danger and one represents opportunity." Although today it is widely recognized that this is not the correct interpretation of the Chinese characters, President Kennedy's wisdom about a crisis yielding unique opportunities may be more important than ever.

Adrienne Janetti

As national security professionals, we spend our days attempting to predict, prevent, and prepare for potential crises across all domains of national security: from political and economic arenas to military and terrorism ones. Crises are generally viewed as dangerous, expensive, and detracting from other agendas and priorities. However, a look back in history illustrates that crises and extreme threats can be useful for directing individuals, a country, and even the world to a solution. As President Kennedy suggested, out of crises can emerge new and incredible opportunities, particularly if traditional approaches and paradigms are questioned and challenged. During a crisis, incentives and motivations change, potentially leading to new cooperative behaviors and even to the creation of new systems or structures. Crises can get the collective adrenaline flowing, focusing minds to solve the problem at hand.

5. BENEFITS OF PAST CRISES

A look back in history quickly reveals numerous ways that crises have offered unexpected benefits for societies, countries, and humanity.

6. RAPID PROBLEM SOLVING AND INNOVATION:

Plato is credited for coining the phrase "Necessity is the mother of invention," and often a crisis acts as the forcing mechanism to compel expeditious innovation, leading to rapid advances in technology, policy, and/or procedures.

- *Deep Water Horizon:* In 2010, the Deep Water Horizon rig exploded and collapsed in the middle of the Gulf of Mexico, unleashing the largest single oil spill in history. This 87-day uncontrolled release of crude oil from the sea floor (over a mile underwater) created an unprecedented problem and an environmental disaster. At the time of the incident, no technology or mechanism existed to contain it. The "Capping Stack" that ultimately brought the release under control—as well as the ability to install it at such great water depth—was developed "on the fly" over a few months. This technology is now incorporated as a contingency for deep water drilling operations across the globe.

Photo credit: U.S. Coast Guard

7. INCREASED RESILIENCY FOR THE NEXT EVENT:

The measures taken to survive and eventually end a crisis often make an organization or country stronger and more resilient for future events.

- *Asian debt crisis 1997-1998*: The Asian financial crisis plunged the affected countries into deep recessions, rapidly increasing unemployment, poverty, and social dislocation. Although devastating for these countries and peoples, especially Indonesia and Thailand, the Asian debt crisis provided valuable financial lessons that would stand Asia in good stead for the global crisis a decade later. Today, many economists agree that the fundamentals of the Asian economies are better than they were in 1997. Among other reforms, Asian economies have built up their foreign exchange reserves as a buffer; most have current account surpluses; and many have allowed their exchange rates to float.

8. NEW LEVELS OF COOPERATION—EVEN AMONG RIVALS:

Large scale crises that challenge multiple interests and equities have a way of pulling together diverse partners—allies and rivals alike—to solve the crisis. If nurtured, these relationships then can be parlayed into cooperation in other areas. *Iraq's invasion of Kuwait:* Iraqi President Saddam Hussein—heavily in debt from his war with Iran—invaded neighboring Kuwait in August 1990, claiming it as his 19th province. Recognizing this as a violation of sovereignty and a challenge to regional allies, the United States under U.N. auspices built and led an unprecedented, multi-national coalition of 32 partners—including the United Kingdom, Russia, Egypt, France, Saudi Arabia, and Syria—to expel Iraqi forces from Kuwait. By January 1991, the coalition had destroyed the Iraqi military, liberated Kuwait, and thwarted Saddam's aims to bring Israel into the conflict and split the coalition. This hallmark of international cooperation, including between the United States and Russia shortly after the end of the Cold War, stands today as the model for successful coalition operations. Furthermore, the Madrid Peace Conference, following the invasion, laid the groundwork for all Middle East-related peace processes attempted since 1991.

9. SYSTEMIC CHANGE:

Global crises that crush existing orders and overturn long-held norms, especially extended, large-scale wars, can pave the way for new systems, structures, and values to emerge and take hold. Without such devastation to existing systems and practices, leaders and populations are generally resistant to major changes and to giving up some of their sovereignty to new organizations or rules.

Thirty Years War: In a Europe torn apart and exhausted by 30 years of religious strife, horrific atrocities, and war, participants negotiated the Peace of Westphalia over five years. Under the terms of the peace settlement, a number of countries received territories or were confirmed in their sovereignty over previously held territories. It also marked the first time complex geopolitical disputes had legal means rather than a default to warfare for conflict resolution. Similarly, the devastation of World War II paved the way for the birth of the United Nations and Bretton Woods institutions, and the 2008 global financial crisis led the major economies to come together to form the G-20.

10. DRAMATIC POLICY SHIFTS:

Sometimes the fear generated from a crisis and corresponding public outcry enables and even forces leaders to make bold and often difficult policy moves, even in countries not involved in or affected by the crisis.

- *Fukushima meltdown*: A massive tsunami hit the northeast coast of Japan in March 2011, causing four of the six nuclear reactors at the Fukushima plant to release radiation into the atmosphere and ocean. Following the Fukushima nuclear disaster, German Chancellor Merkel quickly reversed her position on nuclear energy and surprisingly announced that Germany would gradually shut down all nuclear power plants by 2022. Eight of Germany's 17 plants were closed almost immediately, and Germany launched a long-term plan to make itself independent of both nuclear energy and coal. By 2016, renewables made up almost 30 percent of Germany's gross energy production, and nuclear energy as a percentage of gross energy production dropped from about 23 percent in 2010 to 13.1 percent in 2016.

11. EMERGENCE OF TALENT:

A crisis has a way of letting the cream rise to the top. In the midst of a crisis, those with the right skill sets and talent—even if they are not the identified leaders or top performers—have a way of rising to meet the challenge, creating a dynamic that enables the entire team or group to grow closer and work better together.

The 1999 St. Louis Rams: Pro football player Kurt Warner was cut from the Green Bay Packers in 1994 and took the only job he could, bagging groceries for $5.50/hour at a local store in Iowa. He then spent the next three seasons as an undrafted football player in the B-rated Arena Football and NFL Europe leagues. In 1999, the St. Louis Rams returned from a last place (4-12) finish to start their season in crisis. Their starting quarterback, Trent Green, tore his ACL during a pre-season game, and they were looking down the barrel of another disastrous season. Newly-minted, second-string quarterback Kurt Warner answered the call that season, throwing for 4,353 yards, 41 touchdown passes, and winning 13 games. Then he won the Super Bowl by attempting 45 passes without an interception and throwing two touchdowns for a record 414 yards. Kurt Warner went from supermarket to Super Bowl MVP, and the Rams, a mediocre team at best, coalesced around their unexpected leader to rise to the challenge and beat the odds to transform into world champions.

12. **HEAVY TRAFFIC: INTERNATIONAL MIGRATION IN AN ERA OF GLOBALIZATION**

The American Civil War: Ulysses S. Grant had an unremarkable childhood and mediocre start to his career, showing little promise while at West Point and then repeatedly failing in various business ventures and at farming. He lost significant money (and at one point his house), and had a reputation for bouts of drinking. When the Civil War broke out, he returned to the military, won the Union's first major victory at Fort Donelson, and then captured the city of Vicksburg, Mississippi, breaking the Confederacy's stranglehold on the Mississippi River. After numerous generals failed to turn the tide of the war, President Lincoln appointed Grant to be commander of all U.S. armies, and Grant's creative, diversionary tactics and aggressive, relentless strategy won the war. Reflecting on Grant's career, President Eisenhower said: "He had so many disadvantages going into the 1864 campaign…but he rose to the occasion unlike I've ever seen in American history." And "he (Grant) alone had the determination, foresight, and wisdom" to win.

13. PREPARING FOR THE CRISIS

To be positioned to respond to a crisis and hopefully turn it into an opportunity for growth and positive change, large and often rigid bureaucracies—such as governments and international corporations—can take several steps ahead of time.

14. STUDY AND ANALYZE PREVIOUS CRISES:

Lessons-learned exercises help organizations see what has and has not worked during earlier periods of crisis. Some organizations call it an after-action report while the military calls it a "hot wash." The actual name is less important than the intended effect: to identify what worked well in the crisis and learn for future use. Otherwise, as Winston Churchill famously said, "Those that fail to learn from history are doomed to repeat it." The U.S. intelligence community has utilized such exercises in the wake of the 9/11 attacks and the search for weapons of mass destruction in Iraq to revamp training, create and apply better methodologies, and increase analytic rigor.

15. IMAGINE AND PLAN:

Structured and unstructured scenario exercises help planners imagine and explore the types of crisis—both unexpected and expected—they could face in the near and long term. Examining the origin, trajectory, and consequences of potential crises during a period of calm gives planners a chance to identify bureaucratic weaknesses, establish protocols, acquire resources and capabilities, and develop various responses, while recognizing that "no plan of operations extends…beyond the first contact." Even an outline of a plan helps with initial responses in a crisis situation.

16. ASSEMBLE A MULTI-FACETED TEAM OR NETWORK:

To facilitate a rapid response, key players need to know each other and understand each other's strengths and weaknesses. Getting to know people before a crisis erupt and building relationships help ease personality frictions that would exacerbate the stress of a crisis. It also helps answer the basic question of whom to call across organizations during the immediate crisis response.

17. DEVELOP COMMUNICATION STRATEGY:

Leaders need to pay particular attention to communication strategies—both internally and externally—because words matter, especially during a crisis. Internally, the team or network of people need to have a common lexicon in which to communicate, so that when in crisis mode there is an implicit understanding and agreement that improves efficiency and tamps down stress. In a crisis, if a leader provides what he or she thinks is clear direction, but the team sees as ambiguous, the likelihood of failure becomes significantly higher. Externally, the strategy needs to be focused on managing expectations as well as developing and maintaining public trust. Even successful crisis response can appear to be a failure if the public has lost faith in the system or its leaders.

18. FROM CRISIS TO OPPORTUNITY

Once a crisis is in motion, turning it into an opportunity often requires new ways of seeing, thinking, and responding. Applying traditional responses could lessen the pain temporarily, but often is insufficient to solve the underlying problem. Here are a few approaches for getting to a win in a crisis.

STEP 1: DEFINE THE CRISIS.

The key first step in any crisis is to recognize there is one and not underestimate the severity. The term crisis should not be used casually, because if everything is a crisis, then nothing is a crisis, and such a mentality leads to burnout or delays or ruins resolution. Some crises can easily be defined in advance, while others are a series of events which gradually accrue and lack a clear "this is it" sort of moment. A response team can plan for the obvious crises (e.g. a major terrorist attack, a calamitous natural or man-made disaster, or an accident at a major energy plant), but a crisis that emerges more slowly over a period of time requires responders to stand back to see what is actually happening to know when to call it a crisis.

STEP 2: ASK FUNDAMENTAL QUESTIONS.

As the crisis is unfolding, make sure you understand its nature and process. Is it a linear dynamic with a particular trajectory, or perhaps a reinforcing vicious cycle that needs to be broken? Is there a policy or action contributing to the crisis which could be stopped? Are the right people working on the problem, and do they have access to the right information?

STEP 3: REFRAME THE PROBLEM.

To turn an existing crisis into an opportunity often requires reframing the problem or looking at the issues through a different lens. Reframing could include widening the aperture to see more of the problem. Alternatively, reframing could include bringing in lessons or systems from other domains. For example, medical diagnoses could offer insight for fighting terrorism by using infection patterns of a disease as an analogy for terrorist ideology spreading among a population to identify patient zero or the chief radicalizer.

STEP 4: GIVE PERMISSION TO FAIL.

Often the solution is not immediately obvious but requires many trials and errors. People are more willing to offer needed creative solutions and unique perspectives in an environment that does not penalize its people for taking risks, and sometimes only after everything else fails do the really creative solutions emerge. This is often seen in conjunction with the next recommendation.

STEP 5: MANAGE THE NARRATIVE:

Leaders need to be able to rise above the "management" of a crisis and lead the perception of the event both internally and externally. Getting sufficient buy-in to try new approaches requires trust and confidence in the capabilities and vision of the leadership. When distrust prevails, a crisis can emerge within a crisis. Better leadership of an event provides more latitude to explore opportunities and innovate. For example, after Hurricane Katrina in 2005, local community respect for and trust in Coast Guard Admiral Thad Allen's leadership gave him the opportunity to re-vamp salvage operations, when other civilian leaders were unable to rally the communities behind similar approaches.

19. APPLYING TO CURRENT WORLD CHALLENGES

Several of our most daunting current crises across the globe could benefit from applying aspects of these five steps to help reverse negative forces and promote more positive conditions. There are no obvious, easy, or consensus solutions to these ongoing challenges; thus, the time has come to try to approach them in new ways. New approaches—even on the margins—require challenging deeply held assumptions about how the world works and what are acceptable outcomes. Just providing relief or triaging the situation will not change the underlying cause.

20. CHANGING CLIMATE COULD STIMULATE VIRTUOUS CYCLE.

If the pace and degree of climate change increases dramatically, this global crisis has the potential to catalyze a range of new discoveries, structures, and behaviors—from astonishing technological breakthroughs to unseen levels of global cooperation. The key to begin to address this massive crisis and promote a virtuous cycle of behaviors requires leaders across the globe to apply these steps. First and foremost, all major players need to recognize, define, and take ownership of the problem. As the signs of climate change have increased in the past few years, international cooperation to slow the progression and manage the effects already have increased—albeit slowly. At the Paris climate conference (COP21) in December 2015, 195 countries adopted the first-ever universal, legally binding global climate deal, designed to put the world on track to limit global warming below 2 degrees Celsius above pre-industrial levels. The weather fluctuations of the past year could be the driver to push the international community—allies and rivals alike—to finally implement these programs and even go beyond, but government commitment, both here and abroad, remains in question. To get widespread support for difficult policy changes in energy production, agriculture, and consumption, leaders in the public and private sectors have a responsibility to reframe this crisis as everyone's problem and then develop partnerships to find innovative ways to limit and hopefully, reverse the impact. A modern-day Manhattan project—which concentrated funding, resources, and talent on nuclear weapon development to get ahead of the Germans—could bring the funding and brightest scientific minds together to jump-start creative solutions.

21. MIDDLE EAST CHAOS COULD PROMOTE SYSTEMIC CHANGES.

Multiple scholars have drawn parallels between the Thirty Years War in Europe and today's long-standing wars and conflicts in the Middle East—a region equally riven by religious, ethnic, tribal, and linguistic differences. As the years of destruction in Europe paved the way for the Peace of Westphalia and the beginning of the modern state system, the last six years of upheaval in the Middle East may be the catalyst which finally enables real, systemic change in the region. However, convincing key decision makers inside and outside the region and then launching such a regional revolution may require formally recognizing that parts of the existing regional order have failed and cannot be put back together in their previous form. Moving from collapse to a positive new regional order will require deftly managing the narrative both internally and externally. If such buy-in is achieved, systemic change could take various forms: from major, regional transformation, such as creating more historically authentic state borders or resolving longstanding geopolitical rivalries, to slightly less massive efforts, such as launching a regional initiative for political and economic development.

22. MILLIONS OF REFUGEES COULD FOCUS ATTENTION ON ROOT CAUSES.

Worldwide refugee numbers—caused by genocide, war, famine, and natural disasters—are at their highest levels in recorded history. From Syria to Myanmar to Haiti to sub-Saharan Africa, millions have been displaced within and across borders. Local and international relief organizations have focused on providing short-term relief services or resettling the refugees in their new locations, but these relief organizations are overwhelmed, and efforts are insufficient to address the humanitarian crises. Moreover, the mounting challenges for host countries are having transformational effects on local economies, societies, and political systems. While addressing the unprecedented humanitarian crisis, international efforts from governments, NGOs, and the private sector need to focus more attention on the origins and ongoing drivers of the refugee flows. For example, in 2015 the Association of Southeast Asian Nations (ASEAN) called for member-state parliamentarians to put Myanmar's persecution of the Rohingya (minority Muslim) population as a permanent item on future ASEAN agendas, to build better community relations, and to put permanent external monitors in Myanmar to minimize the violence. All these steps are intended to prevent the deliberate persecution of the Rohingya and their flight to neighboring countries from destabilizing Southeast Asia.[1] Identifying the root causes of refugee flight in each region and country can enable NGOs and governments to focus on the "push" rather than the "pull" factors for refugees, and addressing causes can often be cheaper than managing the implications for years and decades. Many Palestinians have lived outside their ancestral homes for more than 50 years, supported by host countries and United Nations relief agencies. If current causes of population displacement are not addressed and addressed soon, recent and rapidly increasing refugee groups, likewise, could be surviving on what is likely to be dwindling international assistance for successive generations.

23. LEADERSHIP REMAINS THE KEY

Crises are not a prerequisite for innovation or positive change in the world, but major reforms and new paradigms often require the breakdown—generally publicly recognized—of old orders, institutions, and processes. Resolving such crises and charting a more positive trajectory depends in large part on leadership. Leaders are essential to take different and frequently unpopular measures before and during a crisis. Such leaders need courage and humility to first admit the gravity of the challenges at hand and then to develop the apparatus to meet those challenges. Sometimes such crises enable great leaders because the situation changes public mindsets and makes constituents more open and even demanding of change, but in other cases, crises need a leader to step forward and offer a vision and narrative to overcome the challenges. The leader has to take the risk of exploring new, unconventional solutions and dedicate the resources and time to make them happen. The crisis can offer the leader the circumstances and motivation to take great leaps forward, but the leader must grab it. Finding the solutions to our increasingly global and interconnected crises, from terrorism to climate change to refugees, requires this kind of bold and creative leadership.The ability to transform a crisis into an opportunity is the hallmark of all successful enterprises that have stood the test of time. Yet today, even the most successful enterprises are facing crises they've never faced before as they compete in a business environment that is being radically transformed by digitization. It may be a crisis of cost pressure or limited capacity, or the inability to meet the needs of the rapidly changing market. Many large enterprises face strategic challenges that relate to a fragmented IT environment with too much overhead and portfolio maintenance to allow for innovation. And yet there is no time to waste. Action is expected now.

In many of these cases, an enterprise must make a dramatic change to its operating model, which can distress employees and threaten the bottom line. People are not sure of their roles. Leaders are not sure how to turn their vision into a reality.

Enterprises addressing big change often operate as if there are only two extreme approaches:

- The methodical approach, which is a step-by-step way to minimize risk but can take a long time with increased cost and transformation fatigue, or
- The rip-the-bandage-off approach, which focuses on the most important tasks and manages risk in a hyper-care manner. This approach is quick and puts less burden on the organization overall, but the increased risk may cause rework, and—even worse—gaps in service that may come with a high cost.

Lois is speaking at the 2015 ISG Sourcing Industry Conference.
In the best of cases, the answer ends up in between the two extremes, with an approach tailored to specific environmental and internal factors.

Here are the Top 5 ways an enterprise can turn a crisis into an opportunity and implement big change:

1. **Focus on the needs of the business and the customer.**
   Address how the change and its related risks will impact the customer. Identify the most critical roles and activities and develop a more methodical approach in those focus areas, along with enhanced organizational change activities.

2. **Define the burning need.**
   If you were in IT in the year 1999, there was no doubt that the priority was "Y2K." The same clarity can be created today. Identify your priorities and make them known. Build an enterprise-wide understanding of WHY a change is about to take place, WHY it is best for the company and WHY it's best for the IT organization. Everyone has a role to play in making change. Help make it personal for them.
3. **Standardize and integrate processes through an integration platform.**
   Most large enterprises have grown both organically and through mergers and acquisitions. Over time, employees use any number of stopgap solutions to compensate for fragmented and insufficient systems, creating a patchwork of software and manual work-arounds that make for slow and onerous processes. Implement an integration platform that standardizes processes across verticals and train everyone on the same methods.
4. **Build a workforce that offers business-differentiating skills.**
   When an enterprise has a highly tenured workforce, it may become lax, doing things the way they have always been done. This workplace culture can make it difficult to adopt the latest methodologies and emerging technologies. Bring in new and diverse talent to stir in fresh approaches and infuse expertise that may be missing.
5. **Create a strong cross-stakeholder program team to make it happen.**
   Involvement from key vocal business stakeholders, service providers and other adjacent organizations such as finance and procurement is essential for decision-making and progress. Also, be sure to take advantage of those who have done this before. Use tried and true methods. There is no gold medal for making it up on your own.

24. WAYS TO DEAL WITH HARDSHIP

- Entrepreneurs face obstacles from the moment they wake up in the morning, whether they're trying to satisfy investors, struggling to meet payroll, dealing with unexpected complications or delivering a new product to market.

Of course, not everyone is cut out for these rough seas. But some individuals stand out as being particularly well-suited for dealing with what investor and advisor Ben Horowitz calls the "hard things."

It's these entrepreneurs who turn what seems to be an unending stream of difficulty into advantage. They emerge from obstacles stronger and more successful. While others lose their heads (or their shirts), they not only remain calm but seize the offensive and the opportunities. Subjected to such obstacles, these entrepreneurs are transformed much in the way that Andy Grove, former Intel CEO, observed, "Bad companies are destroyed by crisis. Good companies survive them. Great companies are improved by them."

As it turns out, there is a method for understanding and acting upon the obstacles that life throws at us. There is a way to be improved by them. Roman Emperor Marcus Aurelius forged this formula centuries ago and wrote it to himself as a daily reminder:

"Objective judgment, now at this very moment.

Unselfish action, now at this very moment.

Willing acceptance -- now at this very moment -- of all external events.

That's all you need."

Iconic entrepreneurs like John D. Rockefeller, Thomas Edison and Steve Jobs all used this same formula when obstacles confronted them, even using the situation to fueli their immense ambitions. For them, the obstacle was the way.

What follows are five strategies born of this ancient maxim. Forged over centuries, this framework contains timeless wisdom that we all can use to turn the challenges we face into great triumphs for ourselves and our companies. It's the one thing that all great entrepreneurs have in common.

1. Keep a cool head. John D. Rockefeller was barely two years into his first job when the Panic of 1857 struck. Rockefeller could have become depressed and paralyzed by the unfortunate circumstances he faced. But instead of bemoaning the timing of the economic upheaval, he chose to perceive events differently than his peers. He looked at them as an opportunity to learn, to experience a baptism by the market. He was inclined to see opportunity in every disaster, as he once put it.

Within 20 years of that first crisis, Rockefeller alone controlled 90 percent of the oil market.

Like Rockefeller, today's entrepreneurs live in turbulent times. Instead of letting our perception of events cloud our judgment, we can look to companies like LinkedIn and Microsoft, that were both founded during times of economic crisis. When others become lost worrying about a competitor's latest acquisition or an investor having a fit, we can channel Rockefeller's coolness under pressure and look for the opportunity in a crisis.

2. Think differently. Steve Jobs was famous for what observers called his "reality distortion field," which made him dismissive of phrases like "It can't be done." When he ordered a special kind of glass for the first iPhone, manufacturers were aghast at the aggressive deadline. "Don't be afraid," Jobs said. "You can do it. Get your mind around it. You can do it."

Nearly overnight, manufacturers transformed their facilities into glassmaking behemoths, and within six months they had made enough for the whole first run of the phone. His insistence pushed them past what they thought was possible.

We can choose to reject our first judgments and the objections that spring out of them by insisting that obstacles are in fact malleable not concrete. Like, Apple's leader we must have faith in our ability to make something where there was nothing before. To companies like Facebook and Google in their startup years, the idea that no one had ever done something was a good thing. It meant there was an opportunity to own it themselves.

2. Ignore the rules.

Samuel Zemurray, the owner of a small upstart fruit company, was once told he couldn't build the bridge he needed across the river in Central America. This was because government officials had been bribed by United Fruit, one of the most powerful companies in the United States at the time.

So Zemurray had his engineers build two long piers that reached far into the center of the river instead. When needed they strung a temporary pontoon that could connect them in a matter of hours. When United Fruit complained, Zemurray simply laughed and replied, "Why, that's no bridge. It's just a couple old wharfs." We can see this type of stoic ingenuity in startups like Uber and Tesla. There are times that we must take bold action that requires ignorance of outdated or oppressive regulations to accomplish our business goals. What's right is what works.

3. **Anticipate (think negatively).**
   There is a popular technique being used by individuals at startups and Fortune 500 companies that the *Harvard Business Review* has called the pre-mortem. This premortem technique, designed by psychologist Gary Klein, is an exercise in practicing hindsight in advance. But like all great ideas, it's actually nothing new. The credit goes to the ancient Stoics. They even had a better name for it: premeditatio malorum (premeditation of evils).

Our plans rarely resemble the way things turn out. But as stoic entrepreneurs, we can rehearse in our minds what could go wrong and not be caught by surprise. Using this process, we surpass our competitors who are shocked and fall back, devastated by what they did not imagine coming.

4. **Amor fati (or love your fate).**
   When Thomas Edison's entire research and production campus burned to the ground, he didn't get angry or become despondent. Instead, he became energized and invigorated. In only three weeks the factory was partially back up and running, all because Edison practiced what the ancient Stoics called amor fati, love of fate.

In our own lives, we can follow Edison's example when we lose an investor or an employee unexpectedly leaves our startup. When Jack Dorsey was replaced as CEO at Twitter, he didn't become paralyzed or depressed. Instead he accepted it and went on to found Square, one of the largest payment-processing startups in the world. We don't benefit from tears, anger or despair. We always get something out of passionate intensity and energy.

These great entrepreneurs all used strategies from the ancient Stoics to flip obstacles upside and find opportunities within them. They lived out the axioms of Marcus Aurelius and followed a group that Cicero called the only "real philosophers" -- the ancient Stoics -- even if they had never read them.

You might not see yourself as a "philosopher," but then again neither did most of these men and women. They were not academics, but men of action. But the essence of philosophy is action, making good on the ability to turn the obstacle upside down with our minds. Today author and investor Tim Ferriss refers to Stoicism as his "operating system" -- and, in the tradition of those who came before him, he has successfully driven its adoption throughout Silicon Valley. We too can follow his example and use what others see as roadblocks as fuel for our ambitions and inevitable success.

25. IS CRISIS AN OPPORTUNITY?

The word crisis comes from the Greek "to separate, to sift" which means to pass judgment, to keep only what is worthwhile. There is an opportunity in every crisis and the deeper the crisis, the better the opportunity can be. But some people are not capable of seeing it.

26. THE OPPORTUNITY THAT LIES IN EVERY CRISIS...

"We have all heard that the Chinese use the same world to describe the concepts of crisis and opportunity. What they mean to say is that an every crisis lies an opportunity, depending on how it is looked at. The word crisis comes from the Greek "to separate, to sift" which means to pass judgment, to keep only what is worthwhile. There is an opportunity in every crisis and the deeper the crisis, the better the opportunity can be. But some people are not capable of seeing it.
This crisis of gigantic proportions seen by some as the "perfect storm" should help us at least to see better, to see more clearly; to decentralize our look from our individual or national problems; to have a global look; to realize that our local crises (for example the dangerously growing unemployment) cannot be fully understood if we do not place them in an international perspective.

Without being demagogic, because this crisis affects us all and it is not good neither for us nor for the poor, the crisis is giving us an intensive enlightening course. It is letting us see with astonishment how the selfishness and greediness of the rich are producing this great financial crack. We can also see how quickly the global markets react in panic of loosing profits, but also the extraordinary generous measures of the world's governments.

This crisis is astonishing us when we see how efficient the "global fear" is to global bankruptcy in order to mobilize an enormous amount of resources and political efforts; there are so many millions (or billions?) mobilized, that we cannot but compare them to the thin quantities allocated to the urgent policies, wherever they may be, to fight against the poverty that threatens millions in the planet and achieve the humble Millennium Objectives. Poverty also produces fear, global fear, but the poor are used to it; their crisis is the usual one, a "silent tsunami" to which we are used to. And the solidarity reactions are so slow...

Let us be positive. Let us dream that this crisis will enable us to open our eyes a little to make these comparisons. Let us dream that it will have opened many eyes to the need for more ethics and responsibility in the behavior of world economy.

Let us remember this on the eve of Christmas, whose true motivation should not be spending and waste, but the living remembrance of He who said among other provocative things, "One cannot serve God and money".

27. HOW A CRISIS CAN BE BOTH AN OPPORTUNITY AND A DANGER.

Crisis can be either an opportunity or a danger depending on one's perception about a situation .For a child who was placed in foster care due to loss of both parents, crisis would be viewed as danger because of fear of the unknown, lack of trust in the new family, and inability to cope with the present situation. It is only natural for people to perceive crisis to be danger when facing an intense situation. But with the help of the new family and the team members, the child can begin to see opportunities in the crisis. The child can develop the ability to trust and also the ability to control deep emotions .Choose a major crisis (which in some say affected children and adolescents) which occurred in the United States Summarize this crisis, and discuss the trilogy (precipitating event, perception, and failure to cope) which contributed to the crisis.

How to find opportunity in a crisis: 5 ways to create a sense of...

1. Practice **crisis** response. "Make scenario planning part of your DNA." ...
2. Rally the troops. In his book, A Sense of Urgency, Kotter explained that a **crisis**, broadcast clearly to all, can be a call to arms. ...
3. Make the situation clear. ...
4. Step back. ...
5. Beware of post-**crisis** complacency

28. HOW TO FIND OPPORTUNITY IN A CRISIS: 5 WAYS TO CREATE A SENSE OF URGENCY

A crisis can help an IT leader get people's attention in an otherwise noisy environment, says leadership guru John Kotter

In an often volatile, chaotic, and uncertain world, you will face many crises – from small fires to big blowups. Calamity can be disconcerting or downright frightening, but it can also present a chance to make the case for urgency in the technology organization. As leadership guru John Kotter explained to The Enterprisers Project, a crisis can help an IT leader get people's attention in an otherwise noisy environment.

But how do you harness a crisis to help instill a sense of urgency without scaring people or causing them to shut down? Kotter and other experts have tips.

1. PRACTICE CRISIS RESPONSE

"Make scenario planning part of your DNA."
Being prepared for the unexpected makes it more likely that the team can respond with urgency rather than, say, frustration or fear. "Make scenario planning part of your DNA," says Mindy Bostick, global people and change lead at North Highland Worldwide Consulting, who works closely with CIOs and other C-suite executives. "Scenario planning is a great way to bond as a team and get some of those pathways embedded in people's minds so that when they need to respond to a crisis, they can respond calmly. It is only in a calm place that opportunity can be found."

What-if models themselves are also a great way to uncover opportunities generally, says Rajiv Kohli, John N. Dalton Memorial Professor of Business at William & Mary's Raymond A. Mason School of Business.

2. RALLY THE TROOPS

In his book, A Sense of Urgency, Kotter explained that a crisis, broadcast clearly to all, can be a call to arms. But the key is to make the desired response – urgent action – clear, without alarming people.

That requires leaders to themselves demonstrate a response of calm but focused action. The message CIOs should send, Kotter says, is "all hands on deck – we need to deal with this, we have a responsibility to deal with this, we CAN deal with this, and as fast as possible." The aim is to energize and motivate the team to overcome the challenge at hand and suggest that if they address the issue cleverly, they might even uncover the opportunity within the crisis.

3. MAKE THE SITUATION CLEAR

Sometimes a catastrophe is so obvious that it needs little pointing out. But for many organizations, crises may be more like a slow-moving train wreck. In such cases, the organization may be blind to the risk and complacency can set in.

When that is the situation, an IT leader will need to call attention to the hidden but looming danger in a clear and forthright fashion, using relevant data (like market conditions, competitive threats, and related financial or customer information). Honest and transparent communication about the urgent need for change is key, Kotter says.

You need to educate everyone on the rationale for urgency, advises Rob Llewellyn, founder of CXO Transform, which offers a digital transformation framework. "Ensure executives and teams understand why urgency is so important for the initiative," he recently told us. And educate them on the consequences of delayed action as well, he advises.

5. STEP BACK

"You need to have trust that your team will be able to swarm around the problem and come up with solutions."

While it's important for IT leaders to model the urgency response to a crisis, the goal is for the rest of the organization to internalize it. Therefore, they must give their teams the opportunity to rise to the occasion. "As a leader, you need to have trust that your team will be able to swarm around the problem and come up with solutions," Bostick says. "By creating this capability in them, the leader can then feel more confident in taking a step back, taking a bird's eye view, and therefore gaining perspective."

6. BEWARE OF POST-CRISIS COMPLACENCY

There is a difference between urgency and anxious activity. The latter may seem productive and get the organization through the crisis, but it can stress individuals out and ultimately drain them of the energy or excitement the IT leader was hoping to generate.

29. MORE ON LEADERSHIP

- Things leaders with emotional intelligence never do

Finding opportunity in a crisis is not about lighting a fire under the organization to respond to the situation at hand, which can create panic. Instead, it requires a leader to motivate others to think about problems (like the crisis at hand) in new ways. That builds momentum and a more sustainable sense of urgency.

30. WAYS TO CREATE A SENSE OF URGENCY

Gallup grouped the surveyed staff into these three categories:

1. **Engaged Employees** –
   who work with passion and feel a profound connection to their company. They drive innovation and move the organisation forward.
2. **Not Engaged Employees** –
   who are essentially "checked out." They're sleepwalking through their workday, putting time, but not energy or passion, into their work.
3. **Actively Disengaged Employees** –
   who aren't just unhappy at work; they're busy acting out their unhappiness and even undermine what their engaged coworkers accomplish.

People who fall into categories two and three are not what transformation programs need to be successful. In fact, such a lack of commitment at any level of the transformation organization can create unwanted risk from the outset, so it is vital to address it quickly and prevent it from festering. But it takes skilful leadership to move people from categories two and three into one.

The list below provides ideas that can be used to help create a sense of urgency.

1. Custom-build your own strategy for increasing a sense of urgency.
2. Secure stakeholder input and buy-in to the strategy.
3. Don't exhibit panic, stress or loss of control.
4. Make smart decisions with confidence and act on them quickly.

5. Identify obstacles and remove them fast.

6. Establish an outcome-focused culture (instead of task-focused).

7. Evangelize the importance of establishing a sense of urgency.

8. Clarify the consequences of inaction.

9. Identify what works & remove all that doesn't.

10. Identify causes of complacency and how to eradicate them.

31. HOW TO RUN MEETINGS THAT HURT LESS

The human brain constantly scans for threats and rewards. Use these five neuroscience-based tactics to run meetings that are less painful and more productive

How much of your work life do you spend in conference rooms? Making meetings more effective – and quite frankly, less painful – is a top priority for most IT leaders. One answer to improving meeting productivity: Neuroscience. As we begin to understand more about how the brain works, we can see more clues about what we're doing wrong in meetings.

"While you are sitting in a meeting your brain is constantly scanning for threats and rewards. When the threat response occurs in your brain, the innovative, collaborative, parts of your brain shut down," says Dick Axelrod, who with his wife Emily Axelrod co-founded leadership and organizational consultancy The Axelrod Group and co-wrote *Let's Stop Meeting Like This: Tools to Save Time and Get More Done*. "When the reward response occurs in your brain the innovative, collaborative, parts of your brain light up."

Considering how our brains are wired to reward certain behaviors – and to shut down in the face of certain stimuli – can help IT leaders increase the levels of communication, collaboration, and creativity that occur during meetings.

Check out these five neuroscience-inspired actions CIOs can take to promote more productive and less painful meetings.

MAKE THE AGENDA CLEAR

When the human brain registers a threat, it activates the fight or flight response in the primitive emotional center of our brain, the amygdala. When the purpose of a meeting is unclear, that creates such a sense of anxiety, shifting the resources of the brain to survival mode and making problem-solving, communication, and decision-making difficult. Being transparent about the purpose and goals of a meeting increases the likelihood that attendees will arrive engaged and ready to participate rather than being shut down.

"Knowing what you are going to talk about, why, and for long reduces participant anxiety during a meeting by providing a road map for the experience," says Dick Axelrod. "This frees up energy to focus on the issues at hand instead of worrying about what is going to happen next." Some agenda items may themselves, like a budget discussion, may contain a perceived threat, but the value of clarity overall outweighs the risk that like a transparent meeting plan could induce anxiety.

FOSTER A RESPECTFUL ATMOSPHERE

Social threats like humiliation or unfair treatment can have just as damaging an effect on the engagement levels and mental acuity of participants in a meeting. While it's important to have a degree of give-and-take and healthy disagreement within meetings, it's even more critical to ensure that employees are considerate of one another in the process. "Respectful conversations where meeting participants seek to understand differing viewpoints creates psychological safety, which companies like Google have found to be the key component determining group effectiveness," says Emily Axelrod.

"Simple acts like paraphrasing the previous comment before speaking go a long way towards creating a psychologically safe environment, which in turn moves people to the reward state," she says. There are often times in meetings where someone's input must be cut short in consideration of time constraints or sticking to the agenda. Making a point of writing down what they've shared to return to at another time can validate the individual and prevent the social threat response.

BUILD IN BREAKS

It's no coincidence that the solution to a tough problem often comes to us when we're in the shower or exercising – or after we have literally "slept on it."

"Even though you are not directly working on the problem, your brain is running in the background," explains Dick Axelrod. Building in some idle time to let that cognitive magic happen can be beneficial. "While we are not recommending shower breaks, we do recommend building in breaks to get away from a problem so that you can return refreshed," Axelrod says. IT leaders can start a two-hour meeting before lunch and finish it after, for example, or break up an all-day meeting into two half-day sessions with the first half starting in the afternoon and the second portion continuing the following morning.

OFFER STIMULANTS

Buildling challenges into meetings can literally light up attendees' brains and improve their cognitive performance within the meeting. No, we're not talking about coffee. The human brain thrives on a challenge. When someone solves a problem on their own, learns a new skill, or creates a new process, their brain releases a rush of neurotransmitters that can create good feelings associated with the accomplishment. Buildling challenges into meetings can literally light up attendees' brains and improve their cognitive performance within the meeting.

"The trick is to create challenges that stretch the group beyond its current comfort zone," says Emily Axelrod, noting that challenges that are too easy will not engage participants and those that are beyond the skill level of the group will cause them to check out. "If your meeting does not create a challenge that engages meeting participants, energy dissipates as interest wanes."

For some, the challenge of creating a new process is stimulating while for others the challenge of learning something new is more engaging, so the Axelrods suggest building multiple challenges into your meeting to engage the different brains in the room.

GIVE PARTICIPANTS SOME POWER

For many people, a sense of control and active involvement moves their brain toward the reward state. Setting up meetings in a way that allows for some autonomy on the part of attendees can be valuable. "In a meeting, this means being able to have a say about decisions made and the direction the group is going," says Dick Axelrod. "Supporting and encouraging people who take initiative during the meeting reinforces the reward state which opens people up to increased cooperation and new ideas."

11. Exhibit urgency in your body language. Don't shuffle around.

12. Encourage and offer help. Don't nag, bully or threaten.

13. Find reasons to celebrate small successes and communicate them far and wide.

14. Get personal with one-to-one praise. Put your emotional intelligence to work.

15. Agree on deadlines for action.

16. Keep meetings short, to the point, and agenda-driven.

17. Get to the point quickly and encourage others to do the same. Wipe out waffle.

18. Meet your personal deadlines, and expect the same of others.

19. Provide initial guidance and encouragement to get things going.

20. Get peoples' senses involved. Don't just talk and make them read reports.

KOTTER DECLARES THAT A TRUE SENSE OF URGENCY IS RARE

In his book, "A Sense of Urgency," John Kotter explained that a true sense of urgency is rare; mainly because "it is not the natural state of affairs. It has to be created and recreated." So the task of leading a team of people in a transformation at any level will often require an ability to create an atmosphere of urgency that can be embraced, and in turn bring about an atmosphere of achievement.

Kotter offered four fundamental tactics to establish a sense of urgency in any environment:

1. BRING THE OUTSIDE IN

A "we know best" culture reduces urgency; so help people see external opportunities.

2. BEHAVE WITH URGENCY EVERY DAY

Managers and leaders need to walk the talk and lead by example.

3. FIND OPPORTUNITY IN CRISES

A well-leveraged crisis can be a valuable tool to break through complacency.

4. DEAL WITH THE NONOS

Address those who are always working hard to hinder change.

Lead, support and walk the talk
As Kotter and the Gallup poll suggest, a sense of urgency is rare, which is why leaders need to step up and address that fact; because without it, mediocrity prevails and mediocrity is not the stuff that successful transformation is made of. Instead, it's a key ingredient for failure.

MORE ON LEADING TRANSFORMATION

The majority of people who struggle to work independently with a sense of urgency need support. Support to help them feel accountable and committed to achieving their goals, which in turn ignites a sense of urgency in their work. So leaders need to challenge themselves to bring about this change in peoples' hearts and minds – and not sit back declaring that the people around them are not motivated. The ability to move people to being actively engaged with a sense of urgency plays an important role in separating highly effective modern-day leaders from the rest.

32. WAYS TO TURN CRISIS INTO OPPORTUNITY

Personal growth

Are you turning crisis into opportunity? There is little so unsettling as watching fear create the exact experience people were anxious about in the first place. It's called a self-fulfilling prophecy, like when we worry that we won't be able to access toilet paper in a global crisis so we buy all the toilet paper, thereby making toilet paper impossible to find in stores.

"Instead of being fearful, we could be turning crisis into opportunity."

But we have a choice. Instead of being fearful, we could be turning crisis into opportunity. Because good things can happen in hard times, too. Rather than being panicked and afraid, we and our families can get stronger in every way, despite the chaos around us. Here are 5 fast ways to do that.

a. BE A "GLASS HALF FULL" PERSON.

Change is a constant and challenge is, too. So look at what you *can* do instead of at what you *can't* do. Shift from reactive to proactive and from defensive to offensive. When a crisis looms, All Pro Dads are like firefighters or marines, who walk toward the problem instead of cowering away from it.

b. LEARN TO DISTINGUISH BETWEEN WANTS AND NEEDS.

We could complain about the current crisis and what it means for most of us—we have to ration our toilet paper, wait until next year to watch the Olympics, and eat at home instead of at restaurants. But did we ever truly need the conveniences and sources of entertainment that we don't have now? Instead, let's use this as an opportunity to rest more while we can and to reset, reframe, and retool in prep for the future.

c. CULTIVATE A GENEROUS HEART.

Your family needs you. Your community needs you. What can you do to serve them today? Now is the time to be more self-giving than before by being present to your wife and kids, by staying home if you're sick, by giving a roll of toilet paper to the neighbor who ran out. Generosity can be contagious in the family and beyond and it is a far more effective long-term plan than "look out for number one."

d. BUILD BRIDGES.

Social distancing doesn't have to mean isolation. Be proactive in your efforts to stay connected to your loved ones. Video chat with friends and neighbors you can't meet up with like usual. Help your kids have virtual play dates. Call your loved ones who are in nursing homes or assisted living facilities and aren't allowed to have visitors. This will only serve to enhance a sense of community after the immediate crisis passes.

e. BE GRATEFUL FOR THE LESSONS LEARNED.

The National Health Service in the UK reports that, as a group, English schoolchildren were healthier from 1939 through 1952 than in any other time in the 20th Century. The reason? Rationing. More fresh vegetables, food grown at home ,less meat, less candy. Our opportunity in crisis is to look for what's good in the midst of it—the slower pace, the additional family time, the less full schedule—and plan to apply it to our lives when the crisis ends.

33. PHILIPPIANS 3:12-14: STRAINING TOWARD THE GOAL

12 Not that I have already obtained this or am already perfect, but **I press on** to make it my own, because Christ Jesus has made me his
own. 13 Brothers, I do not consider that I have made it my own. But one
thing I do: **forgetting what lies behind and straining forward to what lies ahead**, 14 I press on toward the goal for the prize of the upward call of
God in Christ Jesus.

Post covid 19-turning crisis into opportunities: legal function transformation by New Law

from the COVID-19 crisis that organisations, after focusing on surviving the initial shock of the economic hit and working remotely, are now determining how they could operate their business in the 'new normal'.

For Chief Legal Officers or General Counsels (GCs) who have yet to catch up with legal technology developments over the last decade, COVID-19 should be a wake-up call for many to make significant changes to how they manage and run their legal functions.

One would expect the COVID-19 crisis to change our businesses or business operations in many important ways and this would challenge GCs to think about how this crisis has changed their modus operandi, and what they have learned in the process, so that they can now start preparing for the future.

34. TURNING CHALLENGES INTO OPPORTUNITIES

The story goes that during the Bubonic plague in 1665 Isaac Newton was forced to work from home. He called it the most productive period of his time, developing his theories on calculus, optics and gravity. Today, the ongoing pandemic has changed the dynamics of work for millions. The current crisis is far from positive, but it does open up new opportunities to change your habits and improve wellbeing. Crisis breeds opportunity as they say, and it holds true.

Being forced to adapt to new routines is an opportunity to organize your days differently – to think outside the box and change the paradigm – both personally and in the organization. Saved time from commuting, travel, and chit-chat at the office can be used on the most important tasks for work, family, social or self. Restructuring your days for better life-balance can turn into substantial long-term benefits in all dimensions of your life. What will you start doing differently in and after this crisis?

Below you can find my guidance for staying focused, healthy and even improve your holistic wellbeing while living and working from home:

a. REVISIT YOUR MINDSET AND ATTITUDE

The key to any habit change is having the right mindset. As a former Olympic athlete, my trainer would over and over again drill into me the importance of not being crushed by defeat in one competition. There was always a silver-lining: something to learn, or something to change. The bottom line is: do you feel like a victim in this severe situation, or are you willing to use this as an opportunity to change your habits for the better?

Try to see the benefits of working from home. You can better focus on job tasks, even becoming more productive and increasingly creative. Your colleagues are just a call away. With calendars emptier, you have the opportunity to better stay connected with colleagues, clients and friends.

b. GIVE YOUR NEAR AND DEAR MORE ATTENTION

This is an excellent time to give more attention to or spend more time with family and friends during weekdays. Cherish that: connect with people around you, discuss and listen, learn and observe – and most importantly, invent new routines together to fuel your family and social life. Be creative: I invited my son who's also working from home in another country for a virtual lunch. With one of my clients I proposed a training program, where he used his 4-year-old daughter as a weight in his bodyweight training – they both had a great time bouncing around the living room. I've also heard some of my friends go back to basics by playing cards and board games with their children.

c.. ENJOY THE LUXURY OF SLEEPING AT HOME

If you travel a lot, this is a huge bonus. Long, good quality sleep has a direct impact on your immunity system. Also going to bed earlier has a long-term impact on your wellbeing and performance – something you will start to like!

d. STAY ACTIVE IN A CREATIVE WAY

Even when the venues for many hobbies are closed, there are still many ways to stay active. Use saved commuting time for short exercise bursts, in your living room or outdoors. The internet is now flooded with high quality on-line training programs for strength, mobility, yoga… you name it. If you need to stay inside and space is a limiting factor, focus on strength, for example body-weight training. Add endurance training with skipping ropes or running in place.

35. TURNING OPPORTUNITY INTO ACTION

I recently had a bit of a mid-life crisis. Not a big crisis mind you, more of a little one. But it left me contemplating my life, my future and my work. Rather than run from it, I leaned into it because I have never been afraid to be introspective. Emerging from it, I've learned some interesting things and found some great tools.

One of the tools I used to evaluate my life was called the Golden Circle by Simon Sinek. If you have never heard of it, Google 'Ted talk Golden Circle' or 'Simon Sinek Ted talk' and you will find one of the most watched Ted talks ever. I encourage you to have a watch. It's powerful.

The essence of the Golden Circle is answering three questions:

1. What do you do?
2. How you do you do it?
3. Why do you do what you do?

Most people and most companies can answer the what and the how questions. The more challenging question is the why. Why do you get out of bed? Why do you do what you do? For the sake of what? Why is this important? How do you contribute to others?

Take a moment and contemplate your why. Can you define it?

I've recently spent time contemplating my why. The reason I am telling you this story is my why resulted in changing my business focus.

I have been writing columns for over a decade. One of my first columns was for Produce Plus Magazine and the column was called Persuasive Packaging. I called the column Persuasive Packaging because I believed (and I still believe) packaging is one of the most cost effective, influential and persuasive sales tools you have at your disposal. Especially if you are a smaller grower or marketer.

Branding and packaging, done well, can be a game changer for your business. But a brand and pack are only tactical elements – part of a bigger, strategic picture.

What I have learned over the past few months is…my heart and my skill set lies in strategy. Creating branding and packaging is great fun, but every great brand and pack starts with strategy - seeing new or untapped opportunities and then converting those opportunities to actions that make a difference. A colleague was recently introducing me and she said: ***"what I love about Lisa, is she sees opportunity in divergent things."*** It was a light bulb moment and gave me insight into my why.

While I have not yet landed on the perfect combination of words, my why is about helping people turn opportunity into action so they can achieve more? This explains why I naturally ask questions like, if anything was possible, what would you want to achieve in your business or in your life? For me, it was a-ha moment…and it reframed my thinking.

For me, possibility thinking is all about looking ahead. So, in that spirit, I want you to watch a video. This ad by New Zealand telco Spark came out September 2018. I think it is one of the best, most future-aware ads I have ever seen. From my perspective, this ad paints a very clear picture of the future.

'Generation Voice' changes everything. It is more than Siri. It is more than 'Ok Google.' It puts the power of information into the hands of 'consumers' who only have to be old enough to speak to participate in purchasing and influencing purchases.

CONSIDER THE FOLLOWING:

1. Thing about your own use of voice commands. Are you using voice more/less?
2. Do you have a connected device like Amazon Alexa in your home? What are the primary tasks you give the device?
3. Do you use voice for shopping?
4. What is the potential impact of voice on your business, product or service?

36.

Leadership and rebuilding organizational culture

The U.S. and the rest of the world are dealing with the upheaval from the COVID-19 pandemic and the impact it has had on society and economies. Where do we, as organizational leaders, go from here? This is a complicated situation, with no simple, easy or prewritten solution like "Pandemic Recovery for Dummies." We are in uncharted territory.

The decisions we make now will have impacts on our organizations, workforces and culture for a long time to come. This is an opportunity for HR to take our position as leaders as we begin picking up the pieces and rebuild. There really is no choice but to move forward as a society. Emotional intelligence, communication and leadership are vital to every organization, large or small.

CRITICAL EVALUATION.

At this point, we need to fully understand the needs of the organization and evaluate where we go from here. Do we recall employees? Do we recall small groups of employees over an extended period of time? What about benefits, retirement accounts, accrued days of paid time off? How is the organization doing financially? What can we afford as an organization? By excelling at *Critical Evaluation* and understanding the finances, HR can ensure that logical decisions are made. *Business Acumen* is another competency that HR can utilize from its "seat at the table" throughout the recovery process, playing an extremely important role in strategic decision-making.

- **LEADERSHIP & NAVIGATION.**

There is little choice on this competency. We have to lead our organizations and workforces and navigate them through this evolving situation. Assure people through active listening and follow up on their issues and concerns. Don't be afraid to voice your opinion and push the organization in the right direction. Respect is earned by organizations and leaders, not given. Apply the competency of *Ethical Practice* to guide you.

- **COMMUNICATION, COMMUNICATION, COMMUNICATION**

When cash is tight and the economy is crashing, are there cost-effective solutions to improve gender diversity? Yes, and this is where behavior science solutions can help.

Debiasing organizations using behavioral design interventions can have a large impact on female workforce recruitment, retention, participation, and promotion, often at "shockingly low cost and surprisingly high speed," according to Iris Bohnet, director of the women and public policy program at Harvard University, in the book "What Works: Gender Equality by Design."

Instead of relying on traditional, expensive methods of attempting to teach people about biases with diversity programs that often fail, organizations should focus on changing processes by understanding employee behavior to drive lasting change.

Consider India, a country where women's labor force participation declined from 32% to 21% between 2005 and 2018. Studying gendered demand for jobs in the country, a World Bank report found that one-third of the 800,000 job advertisements in its sample had specified a preferred gender.

Instead of relying on expensive gender bias workshops for recruitment, behavioral science suggests avoiding gendered wordings in job postings so companies can increase the number of women who apply to a job and improve their recruitment pipeline.

Similarly, according to research by Bohnet, women apply to jobs where they satisfy 100% of job requirements while men apply even when they satisfy 65%. Using behavioral science, job ads that separate the "nice-to-have" and "must-have" requirements will improve diversity in the recruitment process.

37. OPINION: HOW COVID-19 COULD HELP CREATE MORE DIVERSITY IN THE AID SECTOR

COVID-19 has created a unique window of opportunity for diversity in global aid. This op-ed explores how to seize it.
Reviewing evidence from behavioral science experiments conducted mostly in developed economy settings and viewing them through the lens of the developing economy context, I developed a gender equity methodology framework for organizations in lower-income countries. The framework

rests on three pillars: setting up systems, recruitment, and promotion and participation. The framework has three rating categories that organizations can use to improve their diversity scores.

COMPONENT

1: STRUCTURES AND PROCESSES

It is difficult to spearhead any change without setting up systems. Set up an equity team with participants across the board of the organization to avoid the equity team becoming a figurehead. Set up gender-disaggregated data systems, as well as sexual harassment prevention and redress systems, and first tackle explicit bias.

Data is a powerful tool to determine the source of inequity in a process. Google, for example, was able to reduce the attrition rate for postpartum women, which data revealed was double that for other employees, by 50%.t's most important headlines in your inbox eInstead, a more effective method is bystander training. This has shown faster and positive effects, in both intent and confidence to intervene, when employees witness any act of sexual harassment taking place around them. It has created allies for survivors and changed the culture of organizations to one of togetherness, instead of alienation, and these effects have lasted even 12 months after training.

RECRUITMENT

This stage aims to close the gender gap in the recruitment process, from job advertisements until final onboarding into the organization.

Opinion: from rhetoric to action — an equity roadmap for the aid community

International NGOs are waking up to the structural racism in our own backyard, according to this op-ed outlining five key approaches to address structural racism and advance equity across the community.
For example, consider employee referrals, a popular incentive used by most companies to receive high-quality applications. While employee referrals are known to be positively correlated with employee satisfaction and tenure, research shows that people network with those like themselves. More often than not, they also refer people like themselves. In an

organization that already has far fewer women than men, employee referrals are a bad strategy to promote gender diversity.

For organizations that blame poor negotiation skills as a factor in the widening gender gap, behavioral science has a simple solution: Reduce ambiguity in negotiation. An intervention as simple as explicitly stating that the salary is negotiable in job ads has been shown to reduce the gender gap in applications by 45%.

38. PARTICIPATION AND PROMOTION

To truly receive the positive impact of a diverse and inclusive workforce, it is not just important to recruit more women, but also to retain and promote them at a rate equal to that of men. Given that recruitment can cost between 16% and 400% of an employee's annual salary, depending on the seniority of the role, it makes business sense for companies to retain the talent they hire.

Start by mapping project allocation to promotion criteria. Because work practices were designed at a time when there were far fewer women than men in the workforce, often the criteria for project allocation and promotion are gendered. Women spend more time than men on building teams or managing crises that are often not recognized. Cumulatively, this sets out a gendered allocation and evaluation process placing women disadvantageously in the company.Intentionally distributing routine administrative tasks that are nonpromotable, instead of asking for volunteers, can neutralize gendered aspects of employee participation.

Behavioral science solutions are as applicable for development sector organizations as they are for corporations. Nonprofits suffer from poor diversity, too: Only 20% of U.S. nonprofits with an annual budget of $50 million or more have female CEOs, gender pay gaps persist, and only 8% of nonprofit executive directors are people of color.If your organization suffers from a lack of diversity, behavioral science solutions will help.Granted, it is hard to mobilize resources and employee time to focus on diversity during a pandemic, but it is in a moment like this that diversity needs to be prioritized. Your diversity and inclusion efforts can predict whether your organization will thrive or crash.Instead of cutting down diversity efforts, look for low-cost solutions to center equity in your organizational processes. Leverage data to track your progress and reap the benefits of a truly diverse and inclusive workforce.

40. IS COVID-19 ,AS A CRISIS,THE END OF THE WORLD AS WE KNOW IT?

David Black - Singapore / Tue, June 23, 2020 / 11:01 am Shoppers wear face masks as a precaution against spreading and contracting COVID-19 while walking past an informational banner on the British government's social distancing guidelines, on June 22, 2020 at an Asda supermarket ourlet in Walthamstow, east London. (AFP/Tolga AKMEN) SHARES If you live in the developed world, the first 20 years of this century might have resembled the apocalypse in slow motion: from SARS to the global financial crisis, from Islamic State to the Sept. 11, 2001 attacks and the War on Terror, from technological disruption to Trumpian anxiety and now, the COVID-19 pandemic. And yet, for many others, the 21st century has also been a revelation: Money to spend, real-time connections with the world, the Babylonian wonders of urban life and much more. Time and again, data and insights have supported this dichotomy. For years, polling and analysis have pointed to growing levels of dissatisfaction and malaise in a number of rich countries. This has been occurring against the backdrop of people who are not only living better lives, but empowered with opportunities thanks to greater mobility and education that have transformed their existence. Our study, World in Crisis, measured the sentiments of citizens from 23 countries toward their governments' COVID-19 crisis management efforts. While the news coverage has focused predominantly on our political findings and how our leaders have performed, these results are in many ways less interesting and largely predictable. What really stood out to us were the wider perceptions of how business, media and communities were seen to have responded. The results of our study, which have been reported in nearly 30 countries to date, show that most countries were rated poorly across the board. The major revelation for me was how people in the majority of the world's most advanced countries – in both the East and the West – were not only shocked and surprised by how quickly the crisis overran their daily lives, but also expressed a wider feeling of being let down, giving the impression that they had expected more. Performance ratings for business leaders and healthcare systems, even local communities and neighborhoods, all scored more poorly in advanced nations. Our findings, from the United States to Italy and to Japan, all point to one thing: People living in wealthier nations feel isolated and vulnerable in a way they have not felt for generations. Of the 11 developed countries and territories covered in the study, only New Zealand scored above average Despite the long-standing evidence from even before our study, we are witnessing a level of denialism, with some commentators suggesting that the scores do not reflect on the best route ahead. The wealthier nations, they argue, just need the time to organize their resources in response to such an unprecedented event. Once this happens, they claim, public opinion will soon shift. Yet the most recent polling in nearly all of these countries indicates that perceptions have actually deteriorated further. Japan and France, for example, scored the lowest in our study, and public opinion in both countries remains anemic. Yet the responses from these countries hardly feel like outliers. South Korea, which scored fourth lowest in our study, even voted overwhelmingly to reelect a president during the crisis. So, in all likelihood, the scores reflect more than simple antagonism towards political leaders. Something else is going on. On the other end, some argue that the countries that scored well are often authoritarian and have leaned on state-controlled media to the extent that their people tell pollsters everything is hunky-dory. While their media diet can have some influence in what people tell pollsters, it does not tell the full picture. Singapore, Thailand and even Iran are all dominated by state media, yet none of them recorded stellar results in our study. Barking up the propaganda tree only gets you so far. Two months on, the vulnerability expressed in our study by people in advanced countries largely remains. It also appears to fit a continuum that has been developing for some time now: the belief and confidence that unraveled after World War II and peaked with the collapse of the Berlin Wall, but was rock solid by the end of the 20th century. The deep global disillusionment reflected so obviously in our poll, as well as in others conducted during the current crisis, has not arisen out of nowhere. It demonstrates a real sense that all is not right. The emotional mindset also goes well beyond anger. There is a growing realization that political and business leaders are short on long-term answers, and "community" is now a term more likely associated with social media than social cohesion. The findings of our study reveals something pertinent: It Is time for developed nations to truly reflect on the way forward. The idea that those living in successful, advanced countries can look forward to perpetual advancement is no longer a given. More and more people are coming to comprehend this. The present crisis, more than all the other recent ones, has laid this bare. With that, confidence can only be regained through new ideas and action. Developed countries need to agree on a new approach to managing the future and a fresh compact with the rest of the world. As with a major war, the pandemic has left everyone with heavy losses, and now is the time to acknowledge that simply trying to paper over long-standing flaws is not going to offer either stability or hope. These new ideas could include rethinking the global institutional framework, whether for trade, health, finance or even technology. Countries also need to reconstitute and develop new forums to include a more diverse representation of key global stakeholders. In the same way that leaders have been forced to address changing attitudes and demands on race and gender in recent years, they now need to expand this change in approach to society itself. So it turns out, once again, that the apocalypse is not nigh. People too often confuse the end times with a reshuffling of the established order. Those who have enjoyed sitting in the premium seats for a long time will have to pay more for them or give them up altogether. As Michael Stipe sang, "It's the end of the world as we know it and I feel fine." *** The writer is founder and CEO of Blackbox Research, a data-driven content and research agency based in Singapore that primarily covers national and regional public opinion. Disclaimer: The opinions expressed in this article are those of the author and do not reflect the official stance of The Jakarta Post. MOST VIEWED MOST ENGAGING US extends GSP status for Indonesia Dozens of tourists show reactive results for COVID-19 during long weekend Indonesia's latest official COVID-19 figures Jokowi condemns Macron's statements on Islam, calls for global unity Challenges of home learning during a pandemic through the eyes of a student Hygiene facilities in Bali's tourist sites to receive facelift amid pandemic How to lose belly fat in seven days Canada sword attacker kills two in Halloween rampage Trump will lose, but it hardly makes a difference Indonesian coal exporters don't expect 'real recovery' until H2 next year

End time

*"End times", "Eschaton", and "Last days" redirect here. For other uses of these terms, see End Times (disambiguation), Endtime (disambiguation), Eschaton (disambiguation), and Last days (disambiguation).*The **end time** (also called **end times**, **end of time**, **end of days**, **last days**, **final days**, **doomsday,** or **eschaton**) is a future described variously in the eschatologies of several world religions (both Abrahamic and non-Abrahamic), which teach that world events will reach a climax.The Abrahamic religions maintain a linear cosmology, with end-time scenarios containing themes

of transformation and redemption. In later Judaism, the term "end of days" makes reference to the Messianic Age and includes an in-gathering of the exiled Jewish diaspora, the coming of the Messiah, the resurrection of the righteous, and the world to come. Some sects of Christianity depict the end time as a period of tribulation that precedes the second coming of Christ, who will face the Antichrist along with his power structure and usher in the Kingdom of God.In Islam, the Day of Judgement is preceded by the appearance of the al-Masih al-Dajjal, and followed by the descending of Isa (Jesus). Isa will triumph over the false messiah, or the Antichrist, which will lead to a sequence of events that will end with the sun rising from the west and the beginning of the Qiyamah (Judgment day).

Non-Abrahamic religions tend to have more cyclical world-views, with end-time eschatologies characterized by decay, redemption, and rebirth. In Hinduism, the end time occurs when Kalki, the final incarnation of Vishnu, descends atop a white horse and brings an end to the current *Kali Yuga*. In Buddhism, the Buddha predicted his teachings would be forgotten after 5,000 years, followed by turmoil. A *bodhisattva* named Maitreya will appear and rediscover the teaching of *dharma*. The ultimate destruction of the world will then come through seven suns.

Since the development of the concept of deep time in the 18th century and the calculation of the estimated age of the earth, scientific discourse about end times has considered the ultimate fate of the universe. Theories have included the Big Rip, Big Crunch, Big Bounce, and Big Freeze (heat death).

IS THERE SUCH A THING CALLED THE BEGINNING AND THE END OF TIME?

Indian religions

BUDDHISM

Buddhist eschatology and *Maitreya*

There is no classic account of beginning or end in Buddhism; Masao Abe attributes this to the absence of God.

History is embedded in the continuing process of samsara or the "beginningless and endless cycles of birth-death-rebirth"Buddhists believe there is an end to things but it is not final because they are bound to be born again. However, the writers of Mahayana Buddhist scriptures establish a specific end-time account in Buddhist tradition: this describes the return of Maitreya Buddha, who would bring about an end to the world.[4] This constitutes one of the two major branches of Buddhist eschatology, with the other being the Sermon of the Seven Suns. End time in Buddhism could also involve a cultural eschatology covering "final things", which include the idea that Sakyamuni Buddha's dharma will also come to an end

MAITREYA

The Buddha described his teachings disappearing five thousand years from when he preached them, corresponding approximately to the year 4300, since he was born in 623BCE. At this time, knowledge of dharma will be lost as well. The last of his relics will be gathered in Bodh Gaya and cremated.There will be a new era in which the next Buddha Maitreya will appear, but it will be preceded by the degeneration of human society. This will be a period of greed, lust, poverty, ill will, violence, murder, impiety, physical weakness, sexual depravity and societal collapse, and even the Buddha himself will be forgotten.

This will be followed by the coming of Maitreya when the teachings of dharma are forgotten. Maitreya was the first Bodhisattva around whom a cult developed, in approximately the 3rd century CE

The earliest known mention of Maitreya occurs in the Cakavatti, or Sihanada Sutta in Digha Nikaya 26 of the Pali Canon. In it, Gautama Buddha predicted his teachings of dharma would be forgotten after 5,000 years.

"At that period, brethren, there will arise in the world an Exalted One named Maitreya, Fully Awakened, abounding in wisdom and goodness, happy, with knowledge of the worlds, unsurpassed as a guide to mortals willing to be led, a teacher for gods and men, an Exalted One, a Buddha, even as I am now. He, by himself, will thoroughly know and see, as it were face to face, this universe, with Its worlds of the spirits, Its Brahmas and Its Maras, and Its world of recluses and Brahmins, of princes and peoples, even as I now, by myself, thoroughly know and see them"

–***DIGHA NIKAYA, 26***

The text then foretells the birth of Maitreya Buddha in the city of Ketumatī in present-day Benares, whose king will be the Cakkavattī Sankha. Sankha will live in the former palace of King Mahāpanadā, and will become a renunciate who follows Maitreya.

In Mahayana Buddhism, Maitreya will attain *bodhi* in seven days, the minimum period, by virtue of his many lifetimes of preparation. Once Buddha, he will rule over the Ketumati Pure Land, an earthly paradise sometimes associated with the Indian city of Varanasi or Benares in present-day Uttar Pradesh. In Mahayana Buddhism, the Buddha presides over a land of purity. For example, Amitabha presides over Sukhavati, more popularly known as the "Western Paradise".

Bodhisattva Maitreya from the 2nd-century Gandharan art period

A notable teaching he will rediscover is that of the ten non-virtuous deeds—killing, stealing, sexual misconduct, lying, divisive speech, abusive speech, idle speech, covetousness, harmful intent and wrong views. The ten virtuous deeds will replace them with the abandonment of each of these practices. Edward Conze in his *Buddhist Scriptures* (1959) gives an account of Maitreya:

The Lord replied, 'Maitreya, the best of men, will then leave the *Tuṣita* heavens, and go for his last rebirth. As soon as he is born he will walk seven steps forward, and where he puts down his feet a jewel or a lotus will spring up. He will raise his eyes to the ten directions, and will speak these words: "This is my last birth. There will be no rebirth after this one. Never will I come back here, but, all pure, I shall win Nirvana."'

–***BUDDHIST SCRIPTURES***

Maitreya currently resides in Tushita, but will come to Jambudvipa when needed most as successor to the historic Śākyamuni Buddha. Maitreya will achieve complete enlightenment during his lifetime, and following this reawakening he will bring back the timeless teaching of dharma to this plane and rediscover enlightenment. The Arya Maitreya Mandala, founded in 1933 by Lama Anagarika Govinda, is based on the idea of Maitreya.

Maitreya eschatology forms the central canon of the White Lotus Society, a revolutionary movement during British colonial rule. It later branched into the Chinese underground criminal organization known as the Triad,which exists today as an international underground criminal network.

Note that no description of Maitreya occurs in any other sutta in the canon, casting doubt as to authenticity of the scripture. In addition, sermons of the Buddha normally are in response to a question, or in a specific context, but this sutta has a beginning and an ending, and its content is quite different from the others. This has led some to conclude that the whole sutta is apocryphal, or tampered with.

SERMON OF THE SEVEN SUNS

In his "Sermon of the Seven Suns" in the Pali Canon, the Buddha describes the ultimate fate of the Earth in an apocalypse characterized by the consequent appearance of seven suns in the sky, each causing progressive ruin till the planet is destroyed:

All things are impermanent, all aspects of existence are unstable and non-eternal. Beings will become so weary and disgusted with the constituent things that they will seek emancipation from them more quickly. There will come a season, O monks when, after hundreds of thousands of years, rains will cease. All seedlings, all vegetation, all plants, grasses and trees will dry up and cease to be. ...There comes another season after a great lapse of time when a second sun will appear. Now all brooks and ponds will dry up, vanish, cease to be.

AŇGUTTARA-NIKĂYA, VII, 6.2 PALI CANON

The canon goes on to describe the progressive destruction of each sun. The third sun will dry the Ganges River and other rivers, whilst the fourth will cause the lakes (e.g. Lake Michigan) to evaporate; the fifth will dry the oceans (e.g. the Atlantic Ocean). Later:

Again after a vast period of time a sixth sun will appear, and it will bake the Earth even as a pot is baked by a potter. All the mountains will reek and send up clouds of smoke. After another great interval a seventh sun will appear and the Earth will blaze with fire until it becomes one mass of flame. The mountains will be consumed, a spark will be carried on the wind and go to the worlds of God. ...Thus, monks, all things will burn, perish and exist no more except those who have seen the path.

—***AŇGUTTARA-NIKĂYA, VII, 6.2 PALI CANON***

The sermon completes with the Earth immersed into an extensive holocaust. The Pali Canon does not indicate when this will happen relative to Maitreya.

HINDUISM

Hindu eschatology and Kalki
Further information: Hindu units of time

In Hindu eschatology, time is cyclic and consists of kalpas. Each lasts 4.1–8.2 billion years, which is a period of one full day and night for Brahma, who will be alive for 311 trillion, 40 billion years. Within a *kalpa* there are periods of creation, preservation and decline. After this larger cycle, all of creation will contract to a singularity and then again will expand from that single point, as the ages continue in a religious fractal pattern.]

Within the current kalpa, there are four epochs that encompass the cycle. They progress from a beginning of complete purity to a descent into total corruption. The last of the four ages is Kali Yuga, our current time, which will be characterized by impiety, violence and decay. The four pillars of dharma will be reduced to one, with truth being all that remains.As written in the Gita:

Yadā yadā hi dharmasya glānirbhavati Bhārata
Abhyutthānam adharmasya tadātmānam sṛjāmyaham

Whenever there is decay of righteousness O! Bharata
And a rise of unrighteousness then I manifest Myself!

At this time of chaos, the final avatar, Kalki, endowed with eight superhuman faculties will appear on a white horse. Kalki will amass an army to "establish righteousness upon the earth" and leave "the minds of the people as pure as crystal."

At the completion of Kali Yuga, the next cycle will begin with a new Satya Yuga, in which all will once again be righteous with the reestablishment of dharma. This, in turn, will be followed by epochs of Treta Yuga, Dwapara Yuga and again another Kali Yuga. This cycle will then repeat till the larger cycle of existence under Brahma returns to the singularity, and a new universe is born.

NORSE RELIGION

Norse mythology depicts the end of days as *Ragnarök*, an Old Norse term translatable as "twilight of the gods". It will be heralded by a devastation known as Fimbulvetr which will seize Midgard in cold and darkness. The sun and moon will disappear from the sky, and poison will fill the air. Dead will rise from the ground and there will be widespread despair.

There follows a battle between – on the one hand – the Gods with the Æsir, Vanir and Einherjar, led by Odin, and – on the other hand – forces of Chaos, including the fire giants and jötunn, led by Loki. In the fighting Odin will be swallowed whole by his old nemesis Fenrir.The god Freyr fights Surtr but loses. Víðarr, son of Odin, will then avenge his father by ripping Fenrir's jaws apart and stabbing the wolf in the heart with his spear. The serpent Jörmungandr will open its gaping maw and be met in combat by Thor. Thor, also a son of Odin, will defeat the serpent, only to take nine steps afterwards before collapsing to his own death.

After this people will flee their homes as the sun blackens and the earth sinks into the sea. The stars will vanish, steam will rise, and flames will touch the heavens. This conflict will result in the deaths of most of the major Gods and forces of Chaos. Finally, Surtr will fling fire across the nine worlds. The ocean will then completely submerge Midgard.

After the cataclysm, the world will resurface new and fertile, and the surviving Gods will meet. Baldr, also a son of Odin, will be reborn in the new world, according to Völuspá. The two human survivors, Líf and Lífþrasir, will then repopulate this new earth.

Linear cosmology: Abrahamic religions and Zoroastrianism

Bahá'í Faith

The founder of the Bahá'í Faith, Bahá'u'lláh, claimed he was the return of Christ as well as the fulfillment of prophetic expectations of other religions.The inception of the Bahá'í Faith coincides with Millerite prophesy, pointing to the year 1844. They also believe the Battle of Armageddon has passed and that the mass martyrdom anticipated during the *End Times* had already passed within the historical context of the Bahá'í Faith. Bahá'ís expect their faith to be eventually embraced by the masses of the world, ushering in a golden age.

CHRISTIANITY

Second coming, Christian eschatology, and last judgment

DATE

Some first-century Christians believed Jesus would return during their lifetime. When the converts of Paul in Thessalonica were persecuted by the Roman Empire, they believed the end of days to be imminent.[23] Scholarly consensus would hold that Jesus, and following him the early Christians, understood the endtime as being imminent.

While some who believe in the literal interpretation of the Bible insist the prediction of dates or times is futile, others believe Jesus foretold signs of the end of days. The precise time, however, will come like a "thief in the night" (1 Thess. 5:2). They may also refer to Matthew 24:36 in which Jesus is quoted as saying:

"But concerning that day and hour no one knows, not even the angels of heaven, nor the Son, but the Father only."

41. GREAT TRIBULATION

Main articles: Abomination of desolation and Great Tribulation

In the New Testament, Jesus refers to this period preceding the end times as the "Great Tribulation" (Matthew 24:21), "Affliction" (Mark 13:19), and "days of vengeance" (Luke 21:22).

The Book of Matthew describes the devastation:

When ye therefore shall see the abomination of desolation, spoken of by Daniel the prophet, stand in the holy place, (whoso readeth, let him understand). Then let them which be in Judaea flee into the mountains. Let him which is on the housetop not come down. ...Neither let him which is in the field return back to take his clothes, and woe unto them that are with child. ...For then shall be great tribulation, such as was not since the beginning of the world to this time, no, nor ever shall be. And except those days should be shortened, there should no flesh be saved: but for the elect's sake those days shall be shortened.

— *Matthew 24:15–22*

The resulting chaos will affect pregnancies, newborns, and a scourge will spread throughout the flesh, save for the elect. The vivid imagery of this section is repeated closely in Mark 13:14–20.

The Gospel of Luke describes a complete unraveling of the social fabric, with widespread calamity and war:

Then he said to them, "Nation will rise against nation, and kingdom against kingdom. There will be great earthquakes, and in various places famines and pestilences. And there will be terrors and great signs from heaven. But before all this they will lay their hands on you and persecute you, delivering you up to the synagogues and prisons, and you will be brought before kings and governors for my name's sake. This will be your opportunity to bear witness. Settle it therefore in your minds not to meditate beforehand how to answer, for I will give you a mouth and wisdom, which none of your adversaries will be able to withstand or contradict. You will be delivered up even by parents and brothers and relatives and friends, and some of you they will put to death. You will be hated by all for my name's sake. But not a hair of your head will perish. By your endurance you will gain your lives.

"But when you see Jerusalem surrounded by armies, then know that its desolation has come near. Then let those who are in Judea flee to the mountains, and let those who are inside the city depart, and let not those who are out in the country enter it, for these are days of vengeance, to fulfill all that is written. Alas for women who are pregnant and for those who are nursing infants in those days! For there will be great distress upon the earth and wrath against this people. They will fall by the edge of the sword and be led captive among all nations, and Jerusalem will be trampled underfoot by the Gentiles, until the times of the Gentiles are fulfilled.

"And there will be signs in sun and moon and stars, and on the earth distress of nations in perplexity because of the roaring of the sea and the waves, people fainting with fear and with foreboding of what is coming on the world. For the powers of the heavens will be shaken. And then they will see the Son of Man coming in a cloud with power and great glory. Now when these things begin to take place, straighten up and raise your heads, because your redemption is drawing near."

And he told them a parable: "Look at the fig tree, and all the trees. As soon as they come out in leaf, you see for yourselves and know that the summer is already near. So also, when you see these things taking place, you know that the kingdom of God is near. Truly, I say to you, this generation will not pass away until all has taken place. Heaven and earth will pass away, but my words will not pass away."

—*Luke 21:10–33*

In the Book of Revelation, the "great tribulation" (Rev. 7:14b) refers to a time of affliction upon God's people. Although some scholars see this period as a time of intense suffering immediately before the second coming of Christ or Parousia, other scholars view the "great tribulation" as the period between the first advent of Christ and his second advent at the end of times.[25] The "great tribulation" thus corresponds to the in-between times – a symbolic period of three and a half years between Christ's exaltation and his return to defeat evil.

CATHOLICISM AND ORTHODOXY

The Profession of Faith addresses Catholic beliefs concerning the Last Days.[26] Catholicism adheres to the amillennial school of thought, promoted by Augustine of Hippo in his work *The City of God*.

PROTESTANTISM

Contemporary use of the term *End Times* has evolved from literal belief in Christian **millennialism**. In this tradition, Biblical apocalypse is believed to be imminent, with various current events as omens of impending Armageddon. These beliefs have been put forward by the Adventist movement (Millerites), Jehovah's Witnesses, and dispensational premillennialists. In 1918 a group of eight, well-known preachers produced the London Manifesto, warning of an imminent second coming of Christ shortly after the 1917 liberation of Jerusalem by the British.

MILLENNIALISTS AND AMILLENNIALISTS

The antichrist, BY Lucas Cranach the Elder (1521). Here the Antichrist is shown wearing the triple crown of the Roman papacy.

Protestants are divided between **Millennialists** and **Amillennialists**. Millennialists concentrate on the issue of whether the true believers will see the tribulation or be removed from it by what is referred to as a Pre-Tribulation Rapture.

Amillennialists believe the end times encompass the time from Christ's ascension to the Last day, and maintain that the mention of the "thousand years" in the Book of Revelation is meant to be taken metaphorically (i.e., not literally, or 'spiritually'), a view which continues to cause divisions within evangelical Christianity.

There is a range of eschatological belief in Protestant Christianity. Christian **premillennialists** who believe the End Times are occurring now, are usually specific about timelines that climax in the end of the world. For some, Israel, the European Union, or the United Nations are seen as major players whose roles were foretold in scripture. Within dispensational premillennialist writing, there is the belief that Christians will be summoned to Heaven by Christ at the Rapture, occurring before a "Great Tribulation" prophesied in Matthew 24–25; Mark 13 and Luke 21. The Tribulation is described in the book of Revelation.

"End times" may also refer to the passing of an age or long period in the relationship between man and God.[27] Adherents to this view cite the Second Epistle to Timothy and draw analogies to the late twentieth and early twenty-first centuries.

Post-Exilic Hebrew books of prophecy such as Daniel and Ezekiel are given new interpretations in this Christian tradition, while apocalyptic forecasts appear in the Judeo-Christian Sibylline Oracles which include the Book of Revelation ascribed to John, the apocryphal Apocalypse of Peter, and the Second Book of Esdras.

FUNDAMENTALISTS

Most **fundamentalist** Christians anticipate biblical prophecy to be literally fulfilled. They see current wars, natural disaster and famine as the birth pangs which Jesus described in Matthew 24:7–8 and Mark 13:8. They believe mankind began in the garden of Eden, and point to the Valley of Megiddo as the place where the current world system will terminate, after which the Messiah will rule for 1,000 years.

ADVENTISTS AND MILLERITES

Icon of the Second Coming. Greek, ca. 1700 A.D.

Religious movements which expect that the second coming of Christ will be a cataclysmic event are generally called **adventism**. These have arisen throughout the Christian era, but were particularly common after the Protestant Reformation. Emanuel Swedenborg considered the second coming to be symbolic, and to have occurred in 1757. Along with others, he developed a religious system around the second coming of Christ, disclosed by new prophecy or special revelation not described in the Bible. The **Millerites** are diverse religious groups which similarly rely upon a special gift of interpretation for predicting the second coming.

The difference between the 19th-century **Millerite** and **Adventist** movements and contemporary prophecy is that William Miller and his followers, based on Biblical interpretation, predicted the time of the Second Coming to have occurred in 1844. Contemporary writing of end time has suggested the timetable will be triggered by future wars and moral catastrophe, and that this time of tribulation is close at hand.

Seventh-day Adventists believe Biblical prophecy to foretell an end time scenario in which the United States works in conjunction with the Catholic

Church to mandate worship on a day other than the true Sabbath, Saturday, as prescribed in the Ten Commandments (Exodus 20:8–11). This will bring about a situation where one must choose for or against the Bible as the will of God.

PRETERISM

Another view of the *end times* is preterism. It distinguishes *the time of the end* from *the end of time*. Preterists believe the term *Last Days* (or *Time of the End*) refers to, neither the last days of the Earth, nor the last days of humankind, but the end of the Old Covenant between God and Israel; which, according to preterism, took place when the Temple in Jerusalem was destroyed in 70 CE.

Preterists believe that prophecies—such as the Second Coming, the desecration of the Jewish Temple, the destruction of Jerusalem, the rise of the Antichrist, the Great Tribulation, the advent of The Day of the Lord, and a Final Judgment—had been fulfilled when the Romans sacked Jerusalem and completely destroyed its Temple.

Proponents of *full preterism* do not believe in a coming resurrection of the dead. They place this event (as well as the Second Coming) in the year 70. Advocates of partial preterism do believe in a coming resurrection. Full preterists contend that partial preterists are merely *futurists*, since they believe the Second Coming, the Resurrection, the Rapture, and the Judgment are yet to come.

Many preterists believe first-century Christians experienced the Rapture to rejoin the Christ.

According with Preterism's interpretation of end times, many "time passages" in the New Testament foretell a Second Coming of Christ, with Last Days to take place within the lifetimes of his disciples: Matt. 10:23, Matt. 16:28, Matt. 24:34, Matt. 26:64, Rom. 13:11–12, 1 Cor. 7:29–31, 1 Cor. 10:11, Phil. 4:5, James 5:8–9, 1 Pet. 4:7, 1 Jn. 2:18.

Dispensationalist prophecies

Dispensationalism is an evangelical futurist Biblical interpretation that foresees a series of dispensations, or periods, in which God relates to human beings under different Biblical covenants. The belief system is primarily rooted in the writings of John Nelson Darby and is premillennial in content. The reestablishment of Israel in 1948 provided a major impetus to the dispensationalist belief system. The wars of Israel after 1948 with its Arab neighbors provided further support, according to John F. Walvoord.[29] After the Six-Day War in 1967, and the Yom Kippur War in 1973, it seemed plausible to many Fundamentalist Christians in the 1970s that Middle East turmoil may well be leading up to the fulfillment of various Bible prophecies and to the Battle of Armageddon.

Members of the dispensationalist movement such as Hal Lindsey, J. Dwight Pentecost, John Walvoord, all of whom have Dallas Theological Seminary backgrounds, and some other writers, claimed further that the European Economic Community, which preceded the European Union, would become a United States of Europe, which would in turn become a Revived Roman Empire ruled by the Antichrist. The Revived Roman Empire also figured into the New Testament writers' vision of the future. The fact that in the early 1970s, there were (erroneously thought to be) seven nations in the European Economic Community was held to be significant; this aligned the Community with a seven-headed beast mentioned in Revelation. This specific prophecy has required revision, but the idea of a Revived Roman Empire remains.

Dispensationalism, in contrast to the Millerite Adventist movement, had its beginning in the 19th century, when John Nelson Darby, founder of the Plymouth Brethren religious denomination, incorporated into his system of Biblical interpretation a system of organizing Biblical time into a number of discrete dispensations, each of which marks a separate covenant with God. Darby's beliefs were widely publicized in Cyrus I. Scofield's *Scofield Reference Bible*, an annotated Bible that became popular in the United States.

Since the majority of the Biblical prophets were writing at a time when the Temple in Jerusalem was still functioning, they wrote as if it would still be standing during the prophesied events. According to preterism, this was a fulfillment of the prophecies. However, according to Futurists, their destruction in AD 70 put the prophetic timetable on hold. Many such believers therefore anticipated the return of Jews to Israel and the reconstruction of the Temple before the Second Coming could occur.[30][31]

Post-tribulation pre-millennialists

A view of the Second Coming of Christ as held by post-tribulational pre-millennialists holds that the Church of Christ will have to undergo great persecution by being present during the great tribulation.

Specific prophetic movements
Main article: Great Disappointment

William Miller predicted the end of the world in 1843, known as the Great Disappointment

In 1843, William Miller made the first of several predictions that the world would end in only a few months. As his predictions did not come true (referred to as the Great Disappointment), followers of Miller went on to found separate groups, the most successful of which is the Seventh-day Adventist Church.

Members of the Bahá'í Faith believe Miller's interpretation of signs and dates of the coming of Jesus were, for the most part, correct.[32] They believe the fulfillment of biblical prophecies of the coming of Christ came through a forerunner of their own religion, the Báb. According to the Báb's words, 4 April 1844 was "the first day that the Spirit descended" into his heart.[33] His subsequent declaration to Mullá Husayn-i Bushru'i that he was the "Promised One"—an event now commemorated by Bahá'ís as a major holy day—took place on 23 May 1844. It was in October of that year that the Báb embarked on a pilgrimage to Mecca, where he openly declared his claims to the Sharif of Mecca.[34][35] The first news coverage of these events in the West was in 1845 by *The Times*,[36] followed by others in 1850 in the United States.[37] The first Bahá'í to come to America was in 1892.[34] Several Bahá'í books and pamphlets make mention of the Millerites, the prophecies used by Miller and the Great Disappointment, most notably William Sears's *Thief in the Night*.[38][39][40]

Restorationism (Christian primitivism)

End times theology is also significant to restorationist Christian religions, which consider themselves distinct from both Catholicism and Protestantism.

Jehovah's Witnesses
Eschatology of Jehovah's Witnesses

Former Watch Tower headquarters in Brooklyn. The society made a number of emphatic claims of impending last days and ensuing chaos between 1879–1924.

The eschatology of Jehovah's Witnesses is central to their religious beliefs. They believe Jesus Christ has been ruling in heaven as king since 1914 (a date they believe was prophesied in Scripture) and that after that time a period of cleansing occurred, resulting in God's selection of the Bible Students associated with Charles Taze Russell to be his people in 1919. They also believe that the destruction of those who reject the Bible's message[41] and thus willfully refuse to obey God[42][43] will shortly take place at Armageddon, ensuring that the beginning of the new earthly society will be composed of willing subjects of that kingdom.

The religion's doctrines surrounding 1914 are the legacy of a series of emphatic claims regarding the years 1799, 1874,1878,1914, 1918 and 1925 made in the Watch Tower Society's publications between 1879 and 1924. Claims about the significance of those years, including the presence of Jesus Christ, the beginning of the "last days", the destruction of worldly governments and the earthly resurrection of Jewish patriarchs, were successively abandoned.[In 1922 the society's principal journal, *The Watchtower*, described its chronology as "no stronger than its weakest link", but also claimed the chronological relationships to be "of divine origin and divinely corroborated ... in a class by itself, absolutely and unqualifiedly correct"and "indisputable facts",while repudiation of Russell's teachings was described as "equivalent to a repudiation of the Lord".

The Watch Tower Society has admitted its early leaders promoted "incomplete, even inaccurate concepts".The Governing Body of Jehovah's Witnesses says that, unlike Old Testament prophets, its interpretations of the Bible are not inspired or infallible.Witness publications say Bible prophecies can be fully understood only after their fulfillment, citing examples of biblical figures who did not understand the meaning of prophecies they received. Watch Tower publications often cite Proverbs 4:18, "The path of the righteous ones is like the bright light that is getting lighter and lighter until the day is firmly established" (NWT) to support their view that there would be an increase in knowledge during "the time of the end", as mentioned in Daniel 12:4. Jehovah's Witnesses say this increase in knowledge needs adjustments. Watch Tower publications also say that unfulfilled expectations are partly due to eagerness for God's Kingdom and that they do not call their core beliefs into question.

The Church of Jesus Christ of Latter-day Saints

Members of The Church of Jesus Christ of Latter-day Saints believe there will be a Second Coming of Jesus to the earth at some time in the future. The LDS Church and its leaders do not make any predictions of the actual date of the Second Coming.

According to church doctrine, the true gospel will be taught in all parts of the world prior to the Second Coming.They also believe there will be increasing war, earthquakes, hurricanes, and man-made disasters prior to the Second Coming.Disasters of all kind will happen before Christ comes.Upon the return of Jesus Christ, all people will be resurrected, the righteous in a first resurrection and the unrighteous in a second, later resurrection. Christ shall reign for a period of 1000 years, after which the Final Judgement will occur.

Islam

Diagram of "Plain of Assembly"(*Ard al-Hashr)* on the Day of Judgment, from autograph manuscript of *Futuhat al-Makkiyya* by Sufi mystic and philosopher Ibn Arabi, ca. 1238. Shown are the 'Arsh (Throne of God), pulpits for the righteous (al-Aminun), seven rows of angels, Gabriel (al-Ruh), A'raf (the Barrier), the Pond of Abundance, al-Maqam al-Mahmud (the Praiseworthy Station; where the prophet Muhammad will stand to intercede for the faithful), Mizan (the Scale), As-Sirāt (the Bridge), Jahannam (Hell) and Marj al-Jannat (Meadow of Paradise).

Muslims believe there are three periods before the Day of Judgment, also known as *ashratu's-sa'ah* or *alamatu qiyami's-sa'ah,* with some debate as to whether the periods could overlap.

According to Adnan Oktar, the first period is said to have begun with the death of Muhammad. The second began with the passing of all his Companions, and ended a thousand years later. Another event of the second period was the Tartar invasion, occurring 650 years after Muhammad. The Mongols, led by Hulagu Khan, grandson of Genghis Khan, attacked Baghdad in 1258 AD and brought the Abbasid caliphate to an end. They massacred millions of Muslims, and the water of the river Tigris turned red with blood. A traditional narration also predicted a fire at Madinah in the Hijaz near Busra in Syria, which Islamic scholars believe occurred in 654 AH. Following the second, the third and final period will be heralded by the appearance of the Mahdi.

Sunnis believe the dead will then stand in a grand assembly, awaiting a scroll detailing their righteous deeds, sinful acts and ultimate judgment.Muhammad will be the first to be resurrected. Punishments will include *adhab*, or severe pain and embarrassment, and *khizy* or shame. There will also be a punishment of the grave between death and the resurrection. Several Sunni scholars explain some of the signs metaphorically.

The signs of the coming end time are divided into major and minor signs: Following the second period, the third is said to be marked by the ten major signs known as *alamatu's-sa'ah al- kubra* (The major signs of the end). They are as follows:

1. A huge black cloud of smoke (dukhan) will cover the earth.
2. Three sinkings of the earth, one in the East.
3. One sinking of the earth in the West.
4. One sinking of the earth in Arabia.
5. The false messiah—anti-Christ, Masih ad-Dajjal—shall appear with great powers as a one-eyed man with his right eye blind and deformed like a grape. Although believers will not be deceived, he will claim to be God, to hold the keys to heaven and hell, and will lead many astray. In reality, his heaven is hell, and his hell is heaven. The Dajjal will be followed by seventy thousand Jews of Isfahan wearing Persian shawls.
6. The return of Isa (Jesus), from the fourth sky, to kill Dajjal.[71]
7. *Ya'jooj* and *Ma'jooj* (Gog and Magog), a Japhetic tribe of vicious beings who had been imprisoned by Dhul-Qarnayn, will break out. They will ravage the earth, drink all the water of Lake Tiberias, and kill all believers in their way. Isa, Imam Al-Mahdi, and the believers with them will go to the top of a mountain and pray for the destruction of Gog and Magog. God eventually will send disease and worms to wipe them out.
8. The sun will rise from the West.
9. The *Dabbat al-ard*, or Beast of the Earth, will come out of the ground to talk to people.
10. The second blow of the trumpet will be sounded, the dead will return to life, and a fire will come out of Yemen that shall gather all to Mahshar Al Qiy'amah (The Gathering for Judgment).

Shia*[edit]*

Many of the signs shown above are shared by both Sunni and Shia beliefs, with some exceptions, e.g. Imam Al-Mahdi defeating Al-Masih ad-Dajjal.

Concepts and terminology in Shia eschatology include Mi'ad, the Occultation, Al-Yamani, and Sufyani. In Twelver Shia narrations about the last days, the literature largely revolves around Muhammad al-Mahdi, who is considered by many beliefs to be the true twelfth appointed successor to Muhammad. Muhammad al-Mahdi will help mankind against the deception by the *Dajjal* who will try to get people in to a new world religion which is called "the great deception"

AHMADIYYA

Ahmadiyya is considered distinct from mainstream Islam. In its writing, the present age has been witness to the evil of man and wrath of God, with war and natural disaster. Ghulam Ahmad is seen as the promised Messiah and the Mahdi, fulfilling Islamic and Biblical prophecies, as well as scriptures of other religions such as Hinduism. His teaching will establish spiritual reform and establish an age of peace. This will continue for a thousand years, and will unify mankind under one faith.

Ahmadis believe that despite harsh and strong opposition and discrimination they will eventually be triumphant and their message vindicated both by Muslims and non-Muslims alike. Ahmadis also incorporate the eschatological views from other religions into their doctrine and believe Mirza Ghulam Ahmed falls into this sequence.

JUDAISM

Scroll of Book of Isaiah

In rabbinic literature, rabbis elaborated and explained the prophecies that were found in the Hebrew Bible, along with oral law and rabbinic traditions about its significance. The main tenets of Jewish eschatology, in no particular order, include:

- God will redeem Israel from the captivity that began during the Babylonian Exile in a new Exodus.
- God will return the Jewish people to the Land of Israel.
- God will restore the House of David and the Temple in Jerusalem.
- God will raise up a regent from the House of David, the Jewish Messiah, to lead the Jewish people and the world and to usher in an age of justice and peace.
- Nations will recognize that the God of Israel is the only true god.
- God will resurrect the dead.
- God will create a new heaven and earth.

The idea of a messianic age, an era of global peace and knowledge of the Creator, has a prominent place in Jewish thought, and is incorporated as part of the end of days. A well-known passage from the Book of Isaiah describes this future condition of the world: "They shall beat their swords into plowshares and their spears into pruning hooks; nation will not lift sword against nation and they will no longer study warfare" (2:4). Maimonides (1135–1204) further describes the Messianic Era in the Mishneh Torah: "And at that time there will be no hunger or war, no jealousy or rivalry. For the good will be plentiful, and all delicacies available as dust. The entire occupation of the world will be only to know God; ... the people Israel will be of great wisdom; they will perceive the esoteric truths and comprehend their Creator's wisdom as is the capacity of man. As it is written (Isaiah 11:9): 'For the earth shall be filled with the knowledge of God, as the waters cover the sea.'"

The Zohar[82] maintains that the seven days of the week, based on the seven days of creation, correspond to the seven millennia of creation. The seventh day of the week, the Shabbat day of rest, corresponds to the seventh millennium, the age of universal rest, or the Messianic Era. The seventh millennium begins with the year 6000 AM, and is the latest time the Messiah can come. A number of early and late Jewish scholars have written in support of this, including the Ramban, Isaac Abrabanel, Abraham Ibn Ezra Rabbeinu Bachya, the Vilna Gaon,the Lubavitcher Rebbe,the Ramchal,Aryeh Kaplan and Rebbetzin Esther Jungreis.[91]

RASTAFARI MOVEMENT

Haile Selassie I is viewed. as god incarnate in Rastafarianism

Rastafarians have a unique interpretation of end times, based on the Old Testament and the Book of Revelation. They believe Ethiopian Emperor Haile Selassie I to be God incarnate, the *King of kings* and *Lord of lords* mentioned in Revelation 5:5. They saw the crowning of Selassie as the second coming, and the Second Italo-Ethiopian War as fulfillment of Revelation. There is also the expectation that Selassie will return for a day of judgment and bring home the lost children of Israel, which in Rastafarianism refer to those taken from Africa through the slave trade. There will then be an era of peace and harmony at Mount Zion in Africa.

ZOROASTRIANISM

Zoroastrian eschatology is considered one of the oldest in recorded history. The birth of its founder, Zoroaster, is unknown, with scholarly dates ranging from 6th century BCE to 5,500 years earlier. Pliny the Elder even suggests there were two Zoroasters.However, with beliefs paralleling and possibly predating the framework of the major Abrahamic faiths, a fully developed concept of the end of the world was not established in Zoroastrianism until 500 BCE. The Bahman Yasht describes:

At the end of thy tenth hundredth winter, the sun is more unseen and more spotted; the year, month, and day are shorter; and the earth is more barren; and the crop will not yield the seed. And men become more deceitful and more given to vile practices. They will have no gratitude. Honorable wealth will proceed to those of perverted faith. And a dark cloud makes the whole sky night, and it will rain more noxious creatures than water.

A Manichaean battle between the righteous and wicked will be followed by the Frashokereti. On earth, the Saoshyant will arrive as the final savior of mankind, and bring about the resurrection of the dead.
The *yazata*s Airyaman and Atar will melt the metal in the hills and mountains, which will flow as lava across the earth and all mankind, both the living and resurrected, will be required to wade through it. *Ashavan* will pass through the molten river as if it were warm milk, but the sinful will burn. It will then flow down to hell, where it will annihilate Angra Mainyu and the last vestiges of wickedness.

The righteous will partake of the *parahaoma*, which will confer immortality upon them. Humanity will become like the Amesha Spentas, living without food, hunger, thirst, weapons or injury. Bodies will become so light as to cast no shadow. All humanity will speak a single language, and belong to a single nation with no borders. All will share a single purpose and goal, joining with Ahura Mazda for a perpetual and divine exaltation.

BIBLIOGRAPHY

1. https://www.thejakartapost.com/academia/2020/06/23/is-covid-19-the-end-of-the-world-as-we-know-it.html.
2. http://bit.ly/tjp-android
3. http://bit.ly/tjp-ios

4. *Lopez, Donald S. (2001). The Story of Buddhism. New York. Harper. p. 33. Unlike so many other traditions, the Buddhist scriptures contain no classic account of an end time, an apocalypse, an eschaton.* quoted in: *Netland, Harold; Yandell, Keith (2009). "The Dharma or the Gospel?". Buddhism: A Christian Exploration and Appraisal. Downers*

Grove, Illinois: InterVarsity Press. p. 196. ISBN 9780830838554. Retrieved 7 July 2019.

5. **^** *Abe, Masao (1985). "Buddhist Nirvana – Its Significance in Contemporary Thought and Life". In LaFleur, William R. (ed.). Zen and Western Thought. Library of Philosophy and Religion (reprint ed.). Basingstoke: Macmillan. p. 214. ISBN 9781349069941. Retrieved 7 July 2019. Since there is no God in Buddhism, there is no creation or last judgment, but rather Emptiness. Thus, for Buddhism, history has neither beginning nor end.*
6. **^** *Netland, Harold; Yandell, Keith (2009). Buddhism: A Christian Exploration and Appraisal. Downers Grove, IL: IVP Academic. p. 196. ISBN 9780830838554.*
7. **^** *Birx, H. James (2009). Encyclopedia of Time: Science, Philosophy, Theology, & Culture. Thousand Oaks, CA: SAGE. p. 409. ISBN 9781412941648.*
8. **^** *Bryant, Clifton; Peck, Dennis (15 July 2009). Encyclopedia of Death & Human Experience: 1-. Thousand Oaks, CA: SAGE. p. 422. ISBN 9781412951784.*
9. ^ Jump up to:[a b c d e f] *Hooper, Rev. Richard (20 April 2011). End of Days: Predictions of the End From Ancient Sources. Sedona, AZ. p. 156.*
10. **^** *"Maitreya". Britannica Encyclopedia.*
11. **^** *Sutta Pitaka, Digha Nikaya, Pāli Canon. "Cakkavatti Sutta: The Wheel-turning Emperor". p. 26. Archived from the original on 5 May 2012.*

MIX
Papier aus verantwortungsvollen Quellen
Paper from responsible sources
FSC® C105338

Printed by Books on Demand GmbH, Norderstedt / Germany